Selected
DOG WALKS
in Hampshire and Wiltshire

JOANNE FAIREY & MICHAEL FAIREY

Selected
DOG WALKS
in Hampshire and Wiltshire

JOANNE FAIREY & MICHAEL FAIREY

Mereo Books

1A The Wool Market Dyer Street Cirencester Gloucestershire GL7 2PR
An imprint of Memoirs Publishing www.mereobooks.com

Selected dog walks in Hampshire & Wiltshire

First published in Great Britain in 2018
by Mereo Books, an imprint of Memoirs Publishing

The address for Memoirs Publishing Group Limited can be
found at www.memoirspublishing.com

The Memoirs Publishing Group Ltd Reg. No. 7834348

Typeset in 9/12pt Bembo
by Wiltshire Associates Publisher Services Ltd.
Printed and bound in Great Britain by Biddles Books

CONTENTS

Introduction

A few words of advice

The Country Code

The Walks:

INTRODUCTION

I love walking with our two Golden Retrievers, Dalton and Emjay, and after a long walk, I like nothing better than having a pub lunch and a pint of beer in a beautiful countryside pub, be it by the fire in the winter or outside in the garden in the summer.

This book started when I posted pictures of a pint of beer and our dogs on our walks on Facebook. All my family and friends would comment on how the views looked and where we were, so my dad and I decided we wanted to share the walks that he had devised. My mum would also join us on our walks and bring a flask of coffee and biscuits for when we stopped for a break half way round.

We have been out in every kind of weather doing this book, and no matter how much it rained or how hard the wind blew, we loved it. The views were breathtaking and watching the wildlife exciting. Nothing makes me happier than seeing our dogs enjoying themselves, be it in the fields and streams and even in the mud.

We prefer our dogs off leads to enjoy their walks, so the walks are tailored to allow off-lead walking. There is some road walking involved, but no major roads, only B roads or little-used ones.

A big thank you to my mum, Pauline Fairey, who supplied the refreshments and joined us, and our two beautiful dogs, who are the reason we did the walks.

We do hope you enjoy this book and these walks with your four-legged friends.

Joanne Fairey

A FEW WORDS OF ADVICE

PUBS

We have visited all the pubs we have chosen and found them to be very dog friendly. You may need to travel a little way to find some of them. There are other pubs around the areas that you might want to visit, but we can't tell you if they are dog friendly, so you may need to check.

LIVESTOCK

Keep all dogs on a lead around any livestock. If at any point you feel threatened by cows, let your dogs go and exit the area as soon as possible.

FOOTWEAR AND WALKING STICKS

Good walking boots are a must for countryside walks, as some of the walks can be very muddy. If you are unsteady on your feet, it would be a good idea to buy walking sticks to help you on uneven surfaces.

WILDLIFE & WILDFLOWERS

On our walks we have encountered so much wildlife and many wild flowers.

For instance, at Itchen Wood, you will see a carpet of bluebells in springtime, as on so many other of our walks and wild garlic in spring woods, while oil-seed rape, with its vibrant yellow, can be seen for miles, with a distinctive smell on a hot day.

We have seen a kingfisher and a heron at Shawford and a muntjac deer at Great Wishford, along with a stoat. Buzzards, hares and roe or fallow deer appear on nearly every walk. We have seen red kites at St Mary Bourne and Alresford and Stoford and foxes at Stratford Tony. Look out too for kestrels, little owls and all the different butterflies of summer. These are just a few examples of the wildlife we have seen, but we know that there is so much more out there.

If you like your wildflowers, here is a short list of the ones we have seen: daffodil, forget-me-not, chives, violets, watercress, wild strawberry, bluebells, wood anemones, dog rose, honeysuckle, cowslip, cow parsley, foxgloves, elderflower, snowdrops, orchids and poppies.

TICKS & ADDERS

Adders are active from spring to the autumn. Please be aware of this and if your dog is bitten please take it immediately to the vets.

Ticks can cause Lyme disease, and are very irritating to dogs. You can buy a tick collar or tablet from the vets, which are very good, and a tick remover to get rid of any you find on your dog. Always examine your dog for ticks after a walk.

FIRST AID KIT

I always take a kit with me just in case your dog injures iself.

WATER

Always take water and a bowl for your dog to have a drink on the way round, especially in the summer months.

COOLING COATS

A must in the hotter months. I wet my dogs' coats the night before and put them in the fridge overnight, then the dogs can wear them out on their walk.

SIGNS, STILES AND GATES

- Always read and respect the Country Code (see opposite).
- Be respectful of the countryside and pick up any litter you may have dropped.
- All gates and stiles must be closed after using them.

DISCLAIMER

Please note that while we have made every effort to ensure all information is correct and up to date at the time of going to press, land use and access arrangements, parking, signposting etc may change, so we cannot guarantee that when you do these walks you will find everything as described. You may wish to check relevant websites etc in advance of your walk for details of any changes to access or parking.

THE COUNTRY CODE

Respect other people: consider the local community and other people enjoying the outdoors.

- Leave no trace of your visit, and take your litter home.
- Keep dogs under effective control.
- Plan ahead and be prepared.Follow advice and local signs.

Remember your actions can affect people's lives and livelihoods. Respect the needs of local people and visitors alike – for example, don't block gateways, driveways or other paths with your vehicle.

- When riding a bike or driving a vehicle, slow down or stop for horses, walkers and farm animals and give them plenty of room. By law, cyclists must give way to walkers and horse-riders on bridleways.
- Co-operate with people at work in the countryside. For example, keep out of the way when farm animals are being gathered or moved and follow directions from the farmer.
- Busy traffic on small country roads can be unpleasant and dangerous to local people, visitors and wildlife – so slow down.
- Leave gates and property as you find them and follow paths unless wider access is available.

- A farmer will normally close gates to keep farm animals in, but may sometimes leave them open so the animals can reach food and water. Leave gates as you find them or follow instructions on signs. When in a group, make sure the last person knows how to leave the gates.
- Follow paths unless wider access is available, such as on open country or registered common land (known as 'open access land').
- If you think a sign is illegal or misleading, such as a 'Private – No Entry' sign on a public path, contact the local authority.
- Leave machinery and farm animals alone – don't interfere with animals even if you think they're in distress. Try to alert the farmer instead.
- Use gates, stiles or gaps in field boundaries if you can – climbing over walls, hedges and fences can damage them and increase the risk of farm animals escaping.

PROTECT THE NATURAL ENVIRONMENT

We all have a responsibility to protect the countryside now and for future generations, so make sure you don't harm animals, birds, plants or trees and try to leave no trace of your visit. When out with your dog make sure it is not a danger or nuisance to farm animals, horses, wildlife or other people.

Protecting the natural environment means taking special care not to damage, destroy or remove features such as rocks, plants and trees. They provide homes and food for wildlife and add to everybody's enjoyment of the countryside.

Litter and leftover food doesn't just spoil the beauty of the countryside, it can be dangerous to wildlife and farm animals – so take your litter home with you. Dropping litter and dumping rubbish are criminal offences.

Fires can be as devastating to wildlife and habitats as they are to people and property, so be careful with naked flames and cigarettes at any time of the year. Sometimes controlled fires are used to manage vegetation, particularly on heaths and moors between 1 October and 15 April, but if a fire appears to be unattended then report it by calling 999.

KEEP DOGS UNDER EFFECTIVE CONTROL

When you take your dog into the outdoors, always ensure it does not disturb wildlife, farm animals, horses or other people by keeping it under effective control. This means that you:

- keep your dog on a lead, or close control
- keep it in sight at all times, be aware of what it's doing and be confident it will return to you promptly on command
- ensure it does not stray off the path or area where you have a right of access

Special dog rules may apply in particular situations, so always look out for local signs – for example:

- Dogs may be banned from certain areas that people use, or there may be restrictions, by-laws or control orders limiting where they can go.
- The access rights that normally apply to open country and registered common land (known as 'open access' land) require dogs to be kept on a short lead between 1 March and 31 July, to help protect ground-nesting birds, and all year round near farm animals.

It's always good practice (and a legal requirement on 'open access' land) to keep your dog on a lead around farm animals and horses, for your own safety and for the welfare of the animals. A farmer may shoot a dog which is attacking or chasing farm animals without being liable to compensate the dog's owner.

However, if cattle or horses chase you and your dog, it is safer to let your dog off the lead – don't risk getting hurt by trying to protect it. Your dog will be much safer if you let it run away from a farm animal in these circumstances, and so will you.

Everyone knows how unpleasant dog mess is and it can cause infections, so always clean up after your dog and get rid of the mess responsibly – 'bag it and bin it'. Make sure your dog is wormed regularly to protect it, other animals and people.

THE WALKS

We have devised 20 countryside walks over Hampshire and Wiltshire, three of which we have modified from other sources to improve them.

For each of the walks, we have outlined a short history of the area. We have also included the following:

1. How to get there
2. OS map reference and nearest postcode available.
3. Hand-written maps and location in the county
4. Where to park
5. Route directions
6. Terrain
7. Approximate distance
8. Information on livestock
9. Public houses
10. Veterinary surgery for emergencies
11. Photographs
12. Introduction
13. Advice for dog walkers

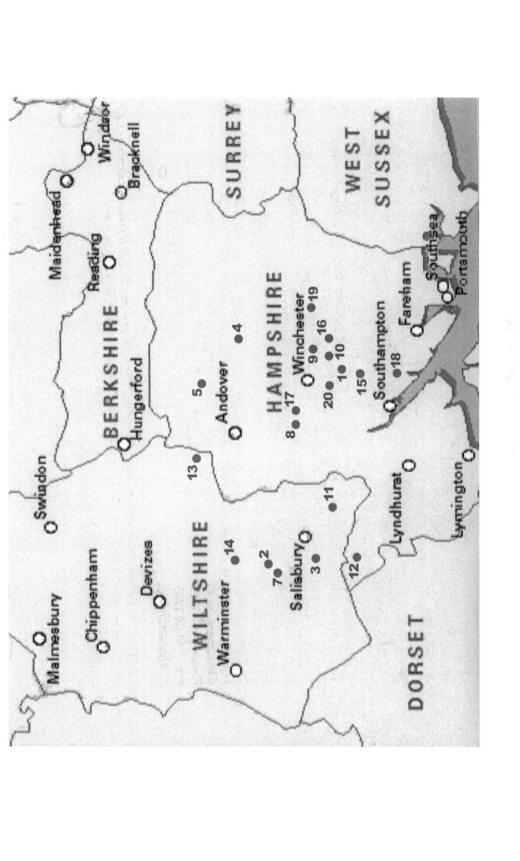

1

MARWELL ZOO/OWSLEBURY

HISTORY:

Owslebury is a small village and parish that lies at the top of a hill on a Roman road from Winchester to the south coast near Porchester. It has a public house, the Ship Inn, a village hall and St Andrew's Church.

Owslebury's claim to fame is for rioting that took place in 1820 among the agricultural workers. This was called the 'swing riots' and was due to the introduction of farm machinery and poor wages. Threshing machines were the first targets and a large mob moved from farm to farm threatening to destroy the agricultural machinery if they were not given money. John Boyes, a local farmer, accompanied the mob, demanding that the farmers and landlords sign an undertaking that they would give two shillings per day to married men and nine shillings per week to single men.

Eventually the rioters were caught and tried, and many were executed in Winchester. John Boyes had many sympathetic followers, so he was transported to Van Diemen's Land, now known as Tasmania. In 1835 the home secretary, Lord Melbourne, pardoned him and he returned home, to continue farming in Owslebury until his death in 1856. A folk song, "The Owslebury lads", recalls the events and can be heard on the CD "Folk songs of Hampshire".

Marwell Zoo has 140 acres of land and was founded by John Knowles in 1972. It was set up for the preservation of animals that are close to extinction. The park is situated on the estate of Marwell Hall and once belonged to the Seymour family, whose famous daughter Jane married Henry VIII. The zoo is now a registered charity and the name is now 'Marwell Wildlife'. It was voted in an online poll of Hampshire residents as the place they were most proud of.

How to get there: Owslebury has Morestead to the north, Baybridge to the east, Fair Oak to the south and Twyford to the west.

- From Morestead, head south on Jackman Hill past Bottom Farm to the T-junction. Turn right onto the main road to Owslebury and pass through the village. Turn right onto Whites Hill and the Ship Inn.

- From Baybridge, head north along Baybridge Lane until you reach a T-junction, turn left and follow road through village. Turn right onto Whites Hill and the Ship Inn.

■ From the south at Fair Oak take the B3037 Mortimers lane. In approx 1.3 miles turn left onto Stroudwood Lane. At the junction turn left onto the B2177. Turn right in approx 0.6 miles onto Hurst Lane. Turn right onto Whaddon Lane and continue until you reach a small green to your left and the Ship Inn.

■ From the west at Twyford, take the Hazely road towards Morestead for approx 1.4 miles, then turn right onto More Lane. Follow this road into Owslebury, ascending Whites Hill to the Ship Inn.

Map Reference:	OS 119 512233
Postcode:	SO21 1LT
Where to park:	Park at or around the Ship Inn pub, making sure not to block any roads
Terrain:	Easy going. Can be very muddy in bad weather.
Distance:	Approx 5¾ miles
Pub:	The Ship Inn. 2 Whites Way, Owslebury, Winchester, SO21 1LT Tel: 01962 777756
Vet:	Unicorn Vets Surgery, Winchester Road, Fair Oak, Eastleigh SO50 7GW Tel: 02380 601900

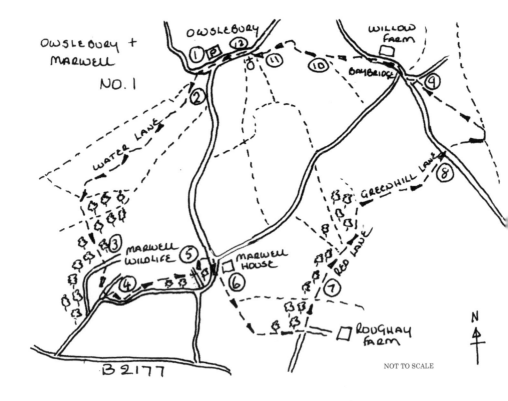

THE WALK

1. With the **Ship Inn** on your right walk down the road. Just after **Boyes Farm**, take a left fork, pass **Longfields**. Look to the left and you will see a **blue badge**, follow the sign.

2. Approx 100 yards down the track it splits into two. Take the sign to the left, which is **Water Lane**. You will come to a T-junction in the woods. Turn left and then follow straight along, ignoring any paths to your left or right. Carry straight up the hill, following the finger signs.

3. At the end of the track you will meet an entrance road which leads to **Marwell Zoo** car park on your right. Cross the road onto a track, following **bridleway** signs. At the bottom of the track you will meet the road going into the entrance to **Marwell Zoo**, go straight across that till you meet another road.

4. Turn left at the road for approx 15 yards and take the track to the left. Walk up the track with **Marwell Zoo** on your left. You are now walking along the perimeter edge of Marwell Zoo. Look out for any of the zoo animals.

5. At the end of the track you will meet an entrance road, and you will see a blue sign that directs you straight across. Follow the blue signs across and come out of the woods following the path around to your left – you may be able to see the zoo's monkeys in front of you. At the end of the track you will meet a road, turn right up the hill past **Lower Baybridge Lane** to your left.

   Carry on going up the hill on the road, and after approx 200 yards at the top of the hill bear left.

6. Pass **Marwell House** on your left and **Marwell Farm House** on the right, which also has a footpath sign. Go along a driveway/track by **Sladford House** and follow footpath signs.

   At the end of the driveway/track, turn right and walk between a fence on your left and a hedge on your right. Keep following the narrow track between bushes and footpath signs. You will meet a stile on your left-hand side, but carry straight on and down the narrow pathway. At the end of narrow track, you will meet another stile. Go over this and straight across towards the gap in the trees. Once you are through, follow the track round left, through the trees.

7. At the end of the track you will come to **Red Lane** (track). Follow the fingerpost and bear left. Go through the barrier and **restricted byway** sign. Keep following the track – do not go left or right.

    At a track junction, carry on the main track. Going right, following the blue marker. Follow the track all the way until you meet **Green Hill Lane** (track). Don't take any lefts or rights.

8. Once you meet the road go slightly right, and you will see a gate/stile on your right. Go over this and straight down the field. You will come to another stile and a sign, **Allan Kingsway.** Go over and continue downhill to another stile and then another. This then goes over onto a track – turn left along that track.

    After approx 85 yards take the fingerpost left, diagonally across the field. At the next stile, in between hedges and a yellow marker post, go over and follow signs diagonally or around the field to the left.

9. At the corner of the field, near a brick garage, is a little decline down onto a road, turn left, down the road. At the bottom of the road it meets another road. Bear right and carry on along that road for approx 400 yards, passing **Coach Cottage** on your right and **Primitive Methodist Church** on you left. Just past **Willow Farm** which is on your right, you will see a fingerpost on your left and a metal gate and stile. Go over and cross the field diagonally.

10. At the first circular gate in the middle of a field, go through until you see the second circular gate. Go through and down to a third circular gate.

    Alternative route: before you get to the 2nd circular gate, walk down right until you get to a track and turn left and walk along until you get to the 3rd circular gate.

11. Once through the 3rd circular gate, go diagonally across the field until you reach a small wrought iron gate. Go through to a swing gate with a **yellow marker**, and once through turn right up a track.

    Carry up the track past agricultural buildings on your left, and up the hill until you meet a lane. Cross the lane and go into **St Andrew's Churchyard**.

12. After going through the churchyard, you will go through a gate and out on to a road. Turn left and walk through **Owslebury village** until you reach the **Ship Inn**, or where you have parked your vehicle.

2

STOFORD

HISTORY:

Stoford is a village in the parish of South Newington, situated by the A360 in the Wylye valley. The most notable building in Stoford is the Swan Inn, which was first in operation in 1740. The name has changed over the centuries from The White Swan to The Swan, The Black Swan and The Swan again from 1993.

Originally Stoford was just a line of farmsteads on the east side of the Warminster road and a ford led from Stoford to Great Wishford across the river. In the early 18th century it was replaced by a bridge which was itself rebuilt in 1841. In the mid-20th century Stoford was enlarged by the building of some 40 residential properties and further building was carried out in the late 20th century.

Some of the original buildings still survive, but only one cottage, as does Stoford house originally built in the

18th century opposite the bridge and is a fine example of an 1822 rebuild.

How to get there: The start of the walk is from the Swan Inn car park in Stoford, which is on the A36 between Salisbury in the south and Warminster in the north.

Map Reference:	OS 130 083356
Postcode:	SP2 0PN
Where to park:	Swan Inn
Terrain:	Moderate, hilly in places
Distance:	Approx 7¾ miles
Pub:	The Swan Inn, Warminster Road, Stoford, Salisbury, SP2 0PR Tel: 01722 790236
Vet:	Avon Lodge Veterinary, 21 Stratford Rd, Salisbury SP1 3JN Tel: 01722 412211

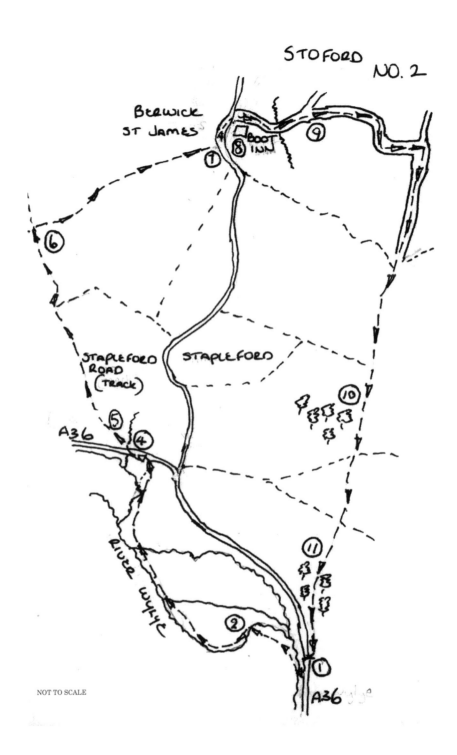

STOFORD NO. 2

BERWICK ST JAMES

BOOT INN

STAPLEFORD ROAD (TRACK)

STAPLEFORD

A36

River Wylye

A36

NOT TO SCALE

10

THE WALK

1. With your back to the **Swan Inn** pub, turn left through
    the car park and turn right over the bridge to **Great
    Wishford**. After you go over the bridge, on your right
    is a gate and a sign for a **public footpath**. Go through
    and follow footpath through the field.

    At the end of the field you will come to a gate. Go through
    this into a smaller field, and straight in front of you is a
    signpost. Go through the gate and turn right.

2. Go over a wooden bridge and through a gate and turn
    left. Following footpath through the field, keep to the
    left of the field, and ignore the bridge to your left. Carry
    on the footpath around the large tree. After following
    the footpath, you will come to a gate. Go through and
    follow footpath straight alongside of the river. This will
    bring you to a stile. Go over and turn to your right, and
    over a small bridge.

    The next bridge leads into field, turn to your left,
    following the footpath sign. You will come to a bridge
    on your left-hand side, ignore that and carry on around
    the field.

    Carry on the footpath, then instead of following the
    river around you have to go straight across the field to
    an opening in the hedges, still following the **footpath
    signs**. This will bring you to a stile, and the next field.

    Follow footpath on the left-hand side, through the field,
    until you reach a walkway with a **yellow marker** on
    it. Go across the walkway and there is a post near the
    middle of the field. Follow the post towards the right-
    hand corner of this field.

3. At the corner of the field go through a hedge and over a wooden bridge. After approx 20 yards is another wooden bridge and little fence - follow the footpath round to the left into a field. You will come to a metal gate, and a stile on your left-hand side. You can get through the gate if it is not locked.

4. Follow along till you get to the main **A36**. On your left is the **Pelican** pub and a river bridge. Cross over the main road and turn left, following the pathway up a small incline.

5. After 100 yards you will come to two houses called **The Little House** and **South House.** There is a track byway between the two houses called **Stapleford Road** (track). Continue up the gravel track.

6. At top of hill on the left-hand side is a slurry store and crossroads. Turn right at the crossroads onto a grassed track. There are **red markers** on the posts. At the end of the byway, which leads out onto a farmyard, carry on down through and past **Berwick Farm Shop** on your right.

7. When you get to the road, turn left and carry along past the cottages through **Berwick St James**.

8. Walk through the village with the **Boot Inn** on your right and a sign post to **Asserton**, then turn right and follow the road along.

    You will walk over a river bridge and through what seems like a smallholding with sheep and birds on your left and houses and barns on your right called **Druids lodge Est. Farm Office.**

9. At the end of the road, it splits into two. Take the right hand fork up the hill. At the top, follow the track round

and through to a tarmac road and between a house on your left and **Beaters Lodge** on your right, then what seems to be a farmer's yard, follow this road until you come to a T-junction, turn right, walk down this road, and you will see a large cow shed on your right, and **Druids Head Farm** on your left. Keep following the path straight, towards woods in the distance.

10. Carry on past the woods, which will now be on your right. You will come to a metal barrier; carry straight on down the grassy hill. There is a sign on a left-hand post. You will meet tracks coming in from the left and right, just continue going straight ahead, following the signs.

11. You then walk down through a little wood. Follow this until you meet the busy **A36**. Cross the road and turn left and you are back to your vehicle.

3

STRATFORD TONY

HISTORY:

Stratford Tony, or Stratford Toney as it is sometimes spelt, is a small village about 4 miles south-west of Salisbury. It lies on the River Ebble and has a church, the Church of St Mary and St Lawrence, which now stands on the site of a previous church dating back to the 14th century. The font, which is 13th century, is believed to be from the original building. The church itself is now part of the Church Conservation Trust. The name Stratford is derived from the Roman road (strat) from Old Sarum to Blandford, which crosses the River Ebble by the ford.

The other part of the name derives from Ralph De Toni, who was a standard bearer for William the Conquer and was given the Manor in 1066. Salisbury racecourse is to the north, whilst high chalk downland extends to the south.

How to get there: Take the A354 to Coombe Bissett. From the north east turn right, just before the Fox and Goose public house, or from the south turn left, just after the Fox and Goose. Turn left onto Drove Lane signposted Bishopstone and continue slightly left onto Stratford Tony road. After approx 1 mile turn left into Stratford Tony and follow the road until you reach a small village green.

Map Reference:	OS 130 093264
Postcode:	SP5 4AT
Where to park:	Park on or near the village green - Do not obstruct any driveway.
Terrain:	Easy to moderately hilly.
Distance:	Approx 6.5 miles.
Pub:	The Fox & Goose, Blandford Road, Coombe Bissett, Salisbury, SP5 4LE. Tel: 01722 718437
Vet:	The Vets, 123 Exeter St, Salisbury SP1 2SG, Tel: 01722 337117

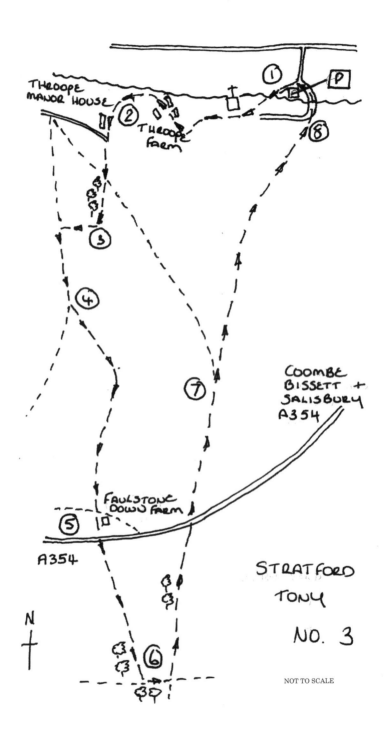

THROOPE MANOR HOUSE

THROOPE FARM

COOMBE BISSETT + SALISBURY A354

FAULSTONE DOWN FARM

A354

STRATFORD TONY

NO. 3

NOT TO SCALE

N

16

THE WALK

1. Head towards the church on the footpath, where you will go over a bridge on the **River Ebble**, and up past **St Mary & St Lawrence Church** on your right. Veer slightly left, and after approx 20 yards you meet another track. Turn right and follow this track until you get to **Throope Farmyard**.

2. Walk through the courtyard with houses to your right. Follow the road all the way round and you will come to a large gate with **Throope Manor House** on your right. Follow this through until you get to a green gate. Continue on the concrete track and restricted byway.

   Go past some large barns on your left-hand side and keep following the concrete track until you see two barns in front of you.

3. At the end, the track turns right up a grass hill footpath, signpost **RESTRICTED BYWAY**. At the top is a metal gate; go through onto a track and turn left.

4. Follow the track until you see gateposts and bear left into **Faulston Drove** (track). Follow the waymark signs. Continue on this track through various gates, ignoring any paths to the left or right until you see a big green barn. Carry straight on till you meet a gate in front of you. Go straight across the lane going down the track. You will pass **Faulstone Farm** barns on your left, and on your right is a weighbridge. This leads down to the **A354**.

5. Cross the main **A354** and there is a hedge dividing two fields. Follow the right-hand side of the hedge all the way down until you meet another hedge. When the hedge is in front of you, go through the gap and head to your left, into a field. Do not go to your right.

   Follow the edge of the field straight down – this leads you onto a track, bear left. There will be a small wood on your right-hand side.

6. At the end of the track is a crossroads. Turn left up along the old drover's road, heading up back towards the **A354.** At the end of the track, when you meet the **A354**, go straight across where there is a track signposted **THROOPE.** Carry on along that track and keep going straight. Halfway along the track, it splits into two – carry on down the right-hand fork.

7. You will come to a track, where you will meet another track coming in from the left. Keep right, following it down the hill.

8. Directly in front of you is the River **Ebble**. Dogs can have a good paddle. Turn right at the river, then sharp left over the bridge back to your car.

4

ITCHEN WOODS

HISTORY:

Itchen Woods has had woodland coverage since the medieval period and contains archaeological features which relate to different spheres of prehistoric life, from burial and settlements to farming and manufacturing tools. The many wooded banks in Itchen Wood represent valuable evidence for the history of woodland management from the medieval period to the present day.

Itchen and Micheldever woods are renowned for the magnificent display in April/May of bluebells, whose fragrance permeates the air.

How to get there: Itchen Woods is off the A33, which runs between Basingstoke in the north and Kingsworthy in the south.

From the south of Kingsworthy take the Basingstoke road. After approx 3.6 miles of dual carriageway is a turning right to Northington & Candovers. Follow the road under the motorway bridge until you see a car parking sign to your left. Carry on for approx 100 yards, where you will see a small car park/track to your right. This is the starting point of the walk.

From the north at Basingstoke, head south on the A33. Go past the turning for Micheldever on your right and take 1st left on the dual carriageway. Follow route as from south above.

Map Reference:	OS 132 529362
Postcode:	Nearest postcode: SO24 9UB
Where to park:	Past Micheldever woods on your left, and approx 100 yards on your right is a small car parking area. Do not block any entrances. If you are unable to park in this small car parking area, return to Micheldever woods car park.
Terrain:	Slight inclines, easy going
Distance:	Approx 5 miles
Pub:	The Northbrook Arms, Stratton Lane Winchester, SO21 3DU Tel: 01962 774150
Vet:	Westpoint Veterinary Group Bridgett's Farm, Bridgett's Lane, Winchester SO21 1AR, Tel: 01962 779593

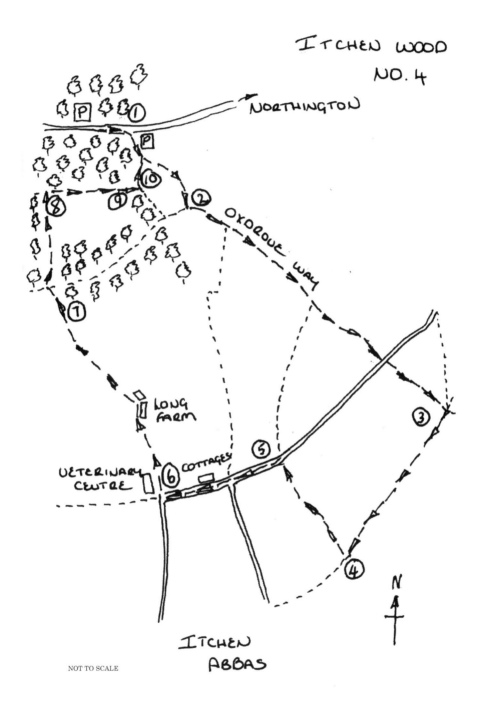

ITCHEN WOOD NO. 4

NORTHINGTON

OXDROVE WAY

LONG FARM

VETERINARY CENTRE

COTTAGES

ITCHEN ABBAS

N

NOT TO SCALE

21

THE WALK

1. From the small car parking area continue straight up the track, not into the woods. Follow the track round to your left, ignoring the track to your right. Ignore the next track on your right and continue straight on.

2. Over the brow of the hill, the track divides. Take the left track as sign posted, until you reach the road. Go under a barrier, cross the road, go under another barrier and continue up the track.

3. Along this track you will meet a track coming in from your left. Walk approx 20 yards and turn right, ignoring paths to your left.

4. Along this track you will come to a large and a small gate on your right. Go through the gate and walk down and then up the side of the field, following the signs until you meet a road.

5. When you get to the road, turn left and walk along the road, passing cottages on your right.

6. At the bottom of the road, turn right and walk up past the **DEFRA/veterinary centre** on your left. Follow track all the way up into the woods, passing **Oxdrove Farmhouse** and **Lone Farm** on your right.

7. When you come to the end of the footpath you will see a green gate in front of you. Go through this and straight ahead.

8. Walk into a small field and carry on until it opens up

to a larger field, then head towards the top left-hand corner, where there is a gate. Go through gate entrance, turn right and walk along the track.

9. At a crossroads on the track, turn left, going down the hill through the woods.

10. At the bottom of the track turn left just before you get to the field. Keep following footpaths so you are walking parallel to this field. The footpath leads you out to the small car park. If your car is parked in the large car park, turn left at the road and walk along for 100 yards on your right.

5

ST MARY BOURNE

HISTORY:

St Mary Bourne stands on the River Bourne, which is a tributary of the Test. The largest watercress company in Europe is located in the village. It has two public houses, the George Inn and the Bourne Valley Inn. The flint and stone church of St Peter is renowned for its Tournai font, which is made from blue-black limestone in the 12th or early 13th century by a mason in the Belgian town of Tournai.

How to get there: From the centre of Whitchurch off the A34, at the roundabout take the second exit into Bell Street if approaching from the south and the third exit if approaching from the north. Continue onto Bloswood Lane. Take the next turn to your right and approx 50 ft after a merging road from your right. Continue on this road until you reach a T- junction with the George Inn on your right. Turn onto the main road and over the bridge, then turn left and follow the road into a car park.

Map Reference:	OS 144 421504
Postcode:	SP11 6BG
Where to park:	In the car park, where there is a village shop
Terrain:	Easy
Distance:	Approx 5 miles
Pub:	The George Inn, The Square, Hurstbourne Tarrant, Andover, SP11 6BG Tel: 01264 738153
Vet:	Foxcotte Veterinary Group, The Old Surgery, 12 St James St, Ludgershall, Andover SP11 9QG, Tel: 01264 790609

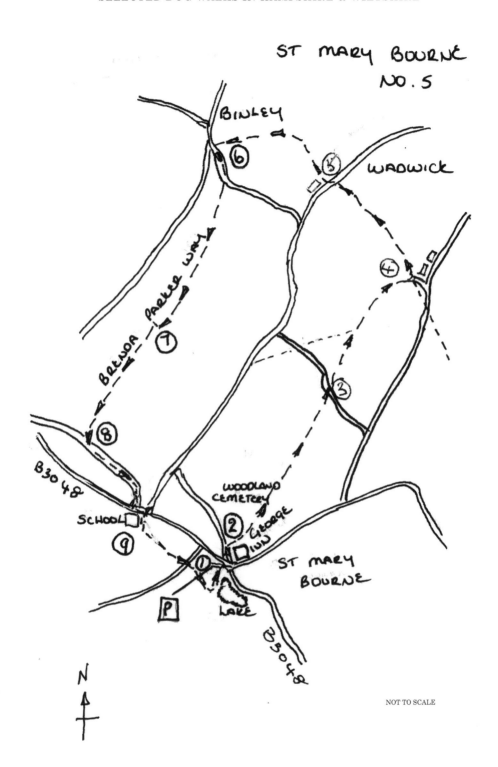

ST MARY BOURNE
NO. 5

NOT TO SCALE

THE WALK

1. Head out of the car park and past the public toilets on your right. This road is called **Bourne Meadows**. Go across the bridge and head for the **George Inn.** Just before the pub turn left up **Spring Hill Lane.**

2. After approx 100 yards and before the 30 mph speed limit sign, on your right-hand side is a footpath. Go up the footpath and on your left-hand side is a **woodland cemetery.** Then pass farm buildings on your right. Continue along the edge of the field until you reach the 1st stile and go across the field, when you will reach a 2nd stile. Go straight across that field (there may be sheep in these fields). You will then come to a 3rd stile, which leads on to a lane.

3. Turn left up the lane, and after a very short walk up, you will see on your right a **fingerpost.** Follow the **yellow way-signs** along the footpath.

   Follow along the edges of fields and between hedges and keep going straight. At the end of the footpath, follow the path across the field.

4. You will then see an opening in the hedge towards some houses. Turn left and go up the track and follow all the way to a road.

5. Once down to the road, turn left and just before the lower Wadwick house is a footpath. Turn right and walk up along it. You will then come to a field. Go straight across the field following the **yellow markers.**

   At the top of the field go through a gap with a bungalow on your right. Go through, then left diagonally across, following **yellow markers.**

6. Follow track down to the road, and then turn left. Take the left road up the hill. Before you hit the bungalow turn right down a track with a signpost **BRENDA PARKER WAY** (Long Hedge Drove). Follow track all the way until it enters a field.

7. Turn right and after approx 20 yards, follow the track left which takes you down to a farmyard, where you then go to the right-hand corner of the yard.

8. This track leads you out onto a quiet road. Turn left along the road and follow it all the way to you meet the **B3048** road.

9. When you come to the main road, go straight across, then turn left past **St Mary Bourne school**, then directly right down **School Lane**. Passing the school, straight ahead is the 1st gate. Go through the 2nd gate and across a field to the 3rd gate. Go through to the 4th gate and cross the road to the 5th gate, then through this field to 6th gate, which leads to the recreation ground and village shop where you parked your vehicle.

6

NEW ALRESFORD

HISTORY:

New Alresford was founded in the 12th/13th century, the idea of Henri de Blois, who was the Bishop of Winchester. The town was expanded by the creation of Old Alresford Pond and the construction of one of the oldest canal systems in England based on the River Itchen. It grew to such a size it sent two members to Parliament, but the Black Death in the 14th century greatly reduced the population. Much of the medieval town was destroyed in the 17th century and much of the town was rebuilt in the 18th century. Many of the Georgian houses remain to this day.

New Alresford is at the south-western end of the 'Watercress Line', which runs steam and diesel trains to Alton, from where you can get a main line train to London. The line got its name due to the watercress that was taken to London. Its official name is the Mid Hants Railway.

How to get there: New Alresford is on the B3047 between Winchester in the west and Bishop Sutton in the east. Follow signs for the Watercress Line.

Map Reference:	OS 132 588325
Postcode:	SO24 9JR
Where to park:	Station Road, off the B3047 leads to the station pay and display car park Other car parking is available in New Alresford, but the time is limited to max 2 hours,
Terrain:	Easy going
Distance:	Approx 6.5 miles
Pub:	Horse & Groom, 2 Broad Street, Alresford, Hampshire, SO24 9AQ. Tel: 01962 734809
Vet:	Cedar Veterinary Group, the Veterinary Surgery, New Farm Rd, Alresford SO24 9QW, Tel 01962 732535

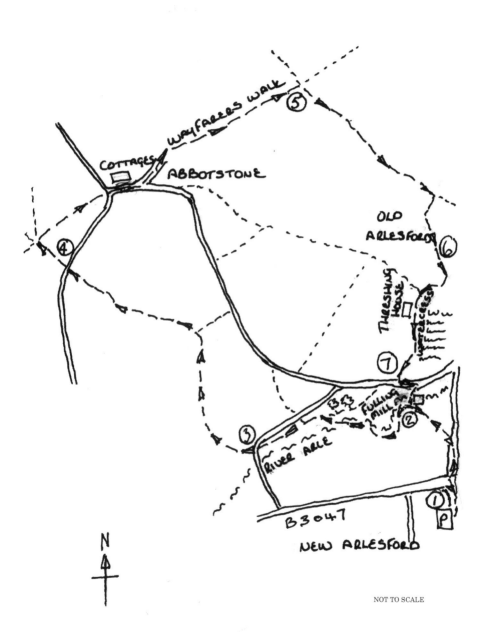

NEW ARLESFORD NO 6

NOT TO SCALE

THE WALK

1. From the **railway car park** head out towards the town centre. When you come to the **B3047** with the **Bell Inn** in front of you, cross over and turn to your right. In approx 100 yards, turn to your left. In the road/pathway is a fingerpost pointing down the road saying **Riverside Walk**. Take the left-hand lane and walk down, and just before the bend on the left-hand side, turn down where the sign says **Riverside Walk**. Follow this lane down, keeping to your right. It then follows the river.

2. Carry on past **Fulling Mill Cottage** over the river – do not go over the bridge, but carry straight on. When you reach a cul sac of the river and a road, follow the river round to you right. On your left will be a sign for **EEL HOUSE & ALRE VALLEY WALK**. At the end of the path you will come up to **the EEL HOUSE** - follow the path around it. Following the **yellow markers**, walk up the hill, where there is a gate, go through the gate and across a driveway to your left and follow pathway until you meet a road.

3. Turn left and walk along the road for approx 50 yards, then you will see a track to your right with a high barrier. At the end of the track you will go under another barrier. Turn to your left, and straight on up the hill passing a cottage on your right. At the end of the track you meet another barrier and a road.

4. Go across the road under another barrier and follow

that track. When you meet a crossroads, along this track turn to your right, where there is a post with a **green arrow**. Follow down the hill under another barrier which leads to a cross roads. Go straight across, passing cottages on your left and take the next turning left towards **ABBOTSTONE FARMHOUSE**. Pass the entrance to **GARDEN COTTAGE**, following the road, which changes to a track, where you will see a fingerpost to your right-hand side which is the **Wayfarer's Walk**. Turn right and follow the track.

Go through the barrier gate and carry along the track, keeping the hedge to you right.

5. After following the hedge along you will come to a derelict farm building on your left. Approx 20 yards past there is a crossroads and a post. Turn right and follow the post signs and the electricity post up the side of the field. When you reach the top right-hand of the field, go through a small opening and carry on following the electricity posts into another field. Carry straight on, go past a storage barn on your left and down the hill, looking to your right, you will see a **yellow marker post**. Turn right and carry along the side of the hedge. Halfway through the field is a gap in the hedge and a **yellow marker**, go through that and follow footpath across the field to the other side.

6. On the other side of the field it will bring you out by a garage area, where you follow the road around past houses. Go past a sign for **THE BROOK**, turning right, then left, ignoring signs to your right. This appears to

be a private road, but carry on past the thatched house called **TRESHING HOUSE** and go straight onto a track and past the cottage on your left.

Follow the **marker post** to your right. Go through a gate until you get to another gate, go through that and into the next field following the track along. Go through an opening and approx 30 yards there is another opening which will bring you out to cottages on your right-hand side. There are **watercress beds** to your left.

7. Follow the track until you reach a road, then turn left, then after approx 150 yards on your right-hand side is an opening. On your right there is a sign saying **FULLING MILL & BYWAY.** Carry on down the track and over the bridge and turn left. Following the footpath brings you back onto the path you first came down. Go to the road and back into the town centre, and retrace your steps back to your vehicle.

7

GREAT WISHFORD

HISTORY:

Great Wishford is a village in the Wylye Valley in Wiltshire, about 5 miles north-west of the city of Salisbury. It was a hamlet before 1066 and its name has evolved over the years from Whichford, Witford, Willesford Magna and Wishford Magna to Great Wishford.

To the south east is Grovely Wood, where the villagers in the 16th century were given the rights to collect wood. To this day the tradition is celebrated on 'Oak Apple Day'. The villagers are woken in the early hours of the morning and at dawn gather oak branches from the woods. They have breakfast in the village pub (the Royal Oak) and then travel to Salisbury, where they dance outside the Cathedral and claim their right inside the Cathedral by shouting 'Grovely, Grovely, Grovely and all Grovely'. In the afternoon there is a formal meal and other events take place in Oak Apple Field. This event take place on May 29th every year.

How to get there: Great Wishford is off the A36 between Salisbury and Warminster. At Stoford take the bridge over the river signposted Great Wishford. Carry straight on until you see a railway bridge and the Royal Oak pub on your left.

Map Reference:	OS 130 077355
Postcode:	SP2 0PD
Where to park:	Park anywhere you can near the Royal Oak pub.
Terrain:	Moderate hills at the start and finish. Fairly easy walk between.
Distance:	Approx 6¼ miles
Pub:	The Royal Oak, Langford Road, Great Wishford, Salisbury SP2 0PD Tel: 01722 790613
Vet:	Cedar Veterinary Group, the Veterinary Surgery, New Farm Rd, Alresford SO24 9QW, Tel 01962 732535

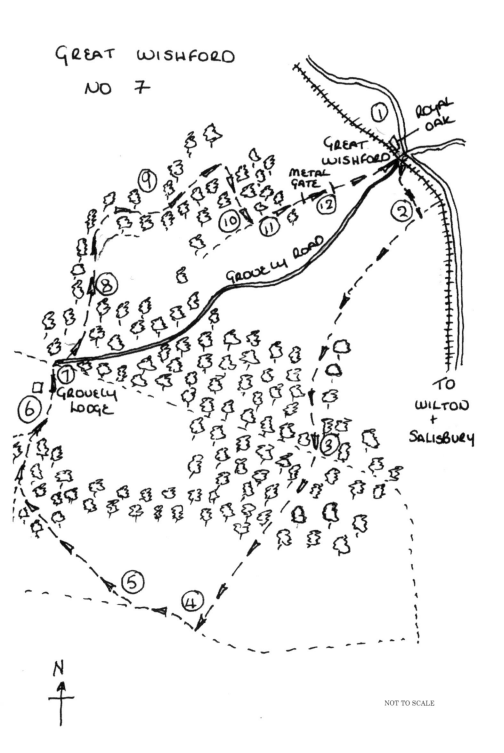

GREAT WISHFORD
NO 7

NOT TO SCALE

THE WALK

1. From the **Royal Oak** pub, look for and go under the railway bridge. Keep walking along the road until you see a track to your left-hand side. Follow the track up the hill, ignoring any stiles on your right.

2. The track goes off down to your left, but turn to your right and pass the barrier. Continue up the track until you come to **Grovely Woods**.

3. Go straight on down this track, and when you come to a tree-lined avenue, go straight across. The tracks narrows and opens up to the country side. Follow this down the hill.

4. At the bottom you will meet a gravel road and a fingerpost on your right saying **restricted byway**. Follow this sign to your right.

5. After a short time, you will see another fingerpost saying **BYWAY**. Turn right, following the sign. Pass the barrier and go up the track and enter the woods.

6. In the woods, keep following the track (don't take right or left) until you meet a gravel road. Follow the gravel road to your right and keep on this byway. This will join up to another gravel road, just carry straight on, passing a barn and **Grovely Lodge** on your left and fields on both sides until you will meet a tarmac road.

7. Turn right down this road, and after approx 130 yards is a track on your left, taking you through the wood.

8. Continue along the track, passing a large field on your right. Follow the outskirts of this field and continue on this track until it branches off to the left.

9. Keep to the main track, ignoring any paths from the left of right, until you come to a clearing on your left and the path branches off to the right. Continue along this path, again ignoring any small paths coming in from the left or right, and then pass another clearing on your left.

10. Continue down until you meet a T-junction, then turn left.

11. After walking on this track, you will see a large gate on your right-hand side. Go into the field and turn left. Walk towards the trees and keep following the grass path through the field until you come across a metal gate.

12. Go through another field, keeping to your right-hand side, until you meet another gate. This will bring you onto a track which takes you down to the road, by the railway bridge. Turn left and go under the railway bridge back to your vehicle.

8

FARLEY MOUNT

HISTORY:

Farley Mount, 4 miles west of Winchester, is one of the highest points in Hampshire and is designated a country park. On top of the mount is a folly which was erected by Paulet St John to honour a horse known as 'Beware chalk pit' which is buried beneath. This name was given him after he fell 25 feet into the chalk pit and then the next year won a race in Worthy down. There are a few folk songs still sung about the folly and the horse. Some excellent views of the Hampshire countryside can be seen from the monument.

How to get there: Farley Mount is to the west of Winchester. From the M3, exit at junction 11 onto A3090 towards Winchester/St Cross. At the roundabout take 2nd exit onto Badger Farm Road A3090 signposted Romsey.

At the next roundabout stay on the A3090. At roundabout take 1st exit onto A3090. Down the hill and turn right onto Enmill Lane. In approx 1.2 miles, at the T-junction, turn right onto Sparsholt Road. At the crossroads turn left signposted Kings Sombourne. Follow this road to a T-junction and then turn right. In approx 0.7 miles turn left into Farley Mount car park.

Map Reference:	OS 132 407293, OS 131
Postcode:	SO21 2JG
Where to park:	Farley Mount Monument car park
Terrain:	Uneven decline near the start and incline into woods.
Distance:	Approx 6¼ miles
Pub:	The Dolphin Inn, Main Road, Hursley, SO21 2JY, Tel: 01962 775209
Vet:	Mildways Veterinary Centre, Easton Lane, Winchester, SO23 7RU Tel: 01962 854088

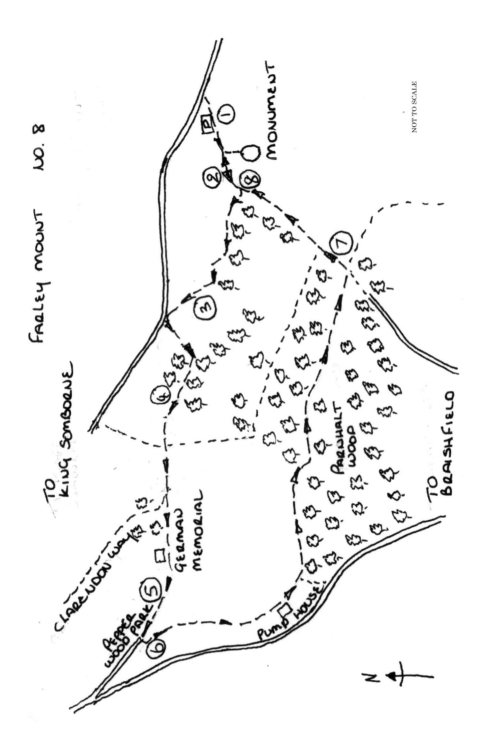

FARLEY MOUNT NO. 8

NOT TO SCALE

MONUMENT

TO KING SOMBOENE

CLARENDON WAY

GERMAN MEMORIAL

PORTER WOOD PARK

PUMP HOUSE

PARNHALT WOOD

TO BRAISHFIELD

N

THE WALK

1. From the car park go up the track and past the barrier. On this track is a turning to your left, which leads up to the Monument.

2. Carry straight along the track and it will split into two, take the left-hand track. At the end of it separates again, left and right.

3. Take the right-hand track and follow it all the way down until it comes to a field – this is the **Clarendon Way**. Follow the footpath across the field. When you reach the corner of that field there is a **fingerpost** pointing left, and a road in front of you. Follow the sign left along the track, all the way until you meet a wood.

4. Walk through the woods and down the hill following the track. Ignore any fingerpost pointing to the left. Continue following the main track and ignoring any fingerposts to your right. This track will take you past a **memorial stone** to four unknown German airmen who died in 1940.

5. The dirt tracks lead out onto a gravel track, which then leads to a tarmac road, passing **Pepperwood Park** on your right. Carry on down that road. After approx 600 yards where there will be a **fingerpost** on your left-hand side, saying **byway**.

6. Turn left and go along this byway, which brings you past the **Pump House** on your right. Follow the track up into **Parnholt Woods**.

7. At the end there is a crossroads – turn left.

8. Carry straight on until you meet the track which you came in on and bear right and walk down back to your car.

9

CHEESEFOOT HEAD

HISTORY:

Cheesefoot Head is a large amphitheatre just outside Winchester, also known as Matterley Bowl. It is situated on the A272 and is a site of special scientific interest. There are three barrows on the site. During the Second World War, many American troops were stationed around the area and the amphitheatre was ideal for boxing events. General Eisenhower addressed his troops here prior to D-Day. The site is used for music festivals now and the most recent was the Boomtown Fair, with more planned for the future.

How to get there: Cheesefoot Head is on the A272 between Winchester and Cheriton. From the M3 junction 9, take the A272 south and onto the A31 going east on the Petersfield road. At the roundabout take the 4th exit then turn left onto the A272. In about 1.2 miles Cheesefoot head car park is on your left. From Cheriton in the east follow the A272 for approx 3.2 miles and Cheesefoot Head car park is on your right.

Map Reference:	OS 132 530276
Postcode:	SO21 1HW
Where to park:	Cheesefoot Head Car park
Terrain:	Slight inclines and declines in places, reasonably easy.
Distance:	Approx 6½ miles
Pub:	Golden Lion, 99 Alresford road, Winchester, SO23 0JZ Tel: 01962 865512
Vet:	Companion Care Vets, inside Pets at Home, Easton Lane, Winchester SO23 7XA, Tel: 01962 843885

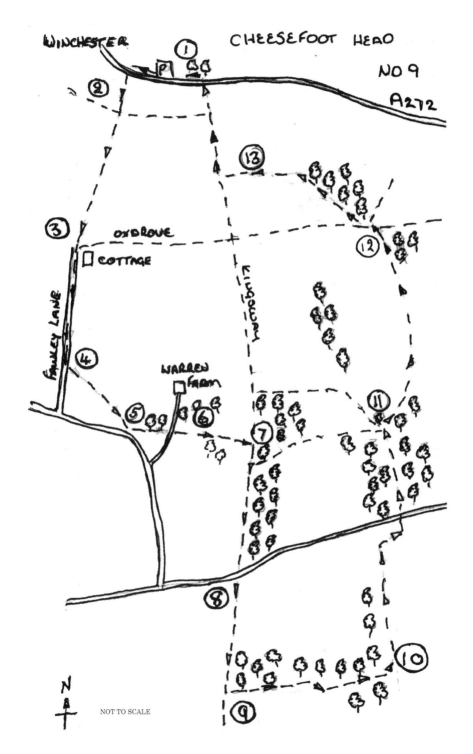

NOT TO SCALE

47

THE WALK

1. At the car park walk towards the road and on your right is a gate. Go through and walk approx 50 yards until you get to an opening onto the **A272** road. Cross over the road and you will see a **fingerpost**, and an opening into a field.

2. Go across the field until you come to another **fingerpost**. This will lead you into a very large field. Follow the pathway straight across the field.

3. At the end of the field it will lead you onto a track, where there is a **waymarker sign**. Follow this track down, passing another track coming in from your left and a cottage.

4. The track leads on to **Fawley Lane**. After approx 100 yards look to your left for a **fingerpost**. It is set back into the hedge, so look carefully. Follow the pathway all the way until you come out onto a road.

5. Turn to your left and follow the road for approx 20 yards, and you will see another track to your left. Follow the **waymarker sign**. At the end of the footpath is another **fingerpost**. Follow it across the farm track. Ignore any of the paths leading off to the left – carry straight on down until you reach another field.

6. You will come across another **fingerpost**. Follow the sign diagonally across and up the field, because of

the **"private property"** sign. At the top you will walk along next to a hedge on your right-hand side, into a small wood. Follow the footpath through the small wood until you come out onto another field. Follow the **waymarker sign** which leads you diagonally across that field.

7. At the corner of the field you will see a fence post/gate, which brings you onto a track, which is the **Kings Way**. Turn right and head down the track. When you see a **fingerpost** carry straight on. At the end of the track you will come to a quiet road.

8. Cross the road into a field and follow the footpath heading towards the right-hand side of the trees in the distance.

9. When you reach the tree line, follow the footpath **waymarker sign**, and after approx 60 yards there is another footpath on your left. There is also a **footpath sign**. Following the edge of the field, bear to your left, with a **waymarker sign** pointing through a wood. Halfway through the wood you will meet a track with a couple of **waymarkers**, go slightly right then left, back into the woods again.

10. At the end of the wood follow **marker signs,** turning left along edge of field. After following the track round the field, you will meet a set of gates. Go around the gates and straight across the road back into woods. Carry straight on down the track.

11. At the end of the track is a **four-way marker post**. Turn right and follow the track through the woods. You will come to another post pointing left; follow this and you will come to a gate. Go through the gate and follow the pathway along the bottom of the field.

12. At the end of this field you will find another gate. Go through and turn left up the track. Follow the signs to the footpath.

13. At the end of the track follow the **waymarkers** and turn left onto a track, back onto the **Kings Way**. At the end of this track, turn right and head straight for the road. This will lead you to a gate. Go through and turn left onto the **A272**. Cross the road and walk on the high footpath. The car park is approx 100 yards on your right.

10

BEACON HILL

HISTORY:

Beacon Hill is a chalk hill in the south Downs and is a site of special scientific interest (SSSI). It is rich in wild flowers and butterflies, many of them very rare. Among the flowers are Man Orchid (*Aceras anthropophorum*), Hairy Rock-Cress (*Arabis hirsuta*) and Rampion (*Phyteuma tenerum*). The rare butterflies include Silver-Spotted Skipper, Chalkhill Blue and Duke of Burgundy. Winchester is 9 miles to the west and there are views of the Isle of Wight and Fawley power station chimney.

The nearest village is Warnford, which lies on the A32 in the Meon valley. It has one church and one pub, which dates back to the 16th century.

How to get there: From Bishop's Waltham take the B3035 east towards Corhampton. At the golf course crossroad turn left onto Beacon Hill Lane. Turn left at the junction and follow the road to the right. The car park is in front of you before the road bears to the left. From Warnford on the A32, go past the George & Falcon and take the 2nd exit on your right onto Wheely Down road for approx 1.6 miles. At the crossroads turn left towards Beacon Hill Lane. Continue onto Beacon Hill Lane for approx 0.5 miles and the car park is on your left before the road bears to the right.

Map Reference:	OS 119 699228
Postcode:	None available
Where to park:	Nature reserve car park.
Terrain:	Steep decline at start. Steep incline after Exton Stud
Distance:	Approx 7 miles
Pub:	The George & Falcon, Warnford Road, Warnford, Hampshire, SO32 3LB. Tel: 01730 829623
Vet:	Animed Veterinary Hospital, Botley Road, Shedfield, Southampton SO32 2JG, tel: 01329 833112

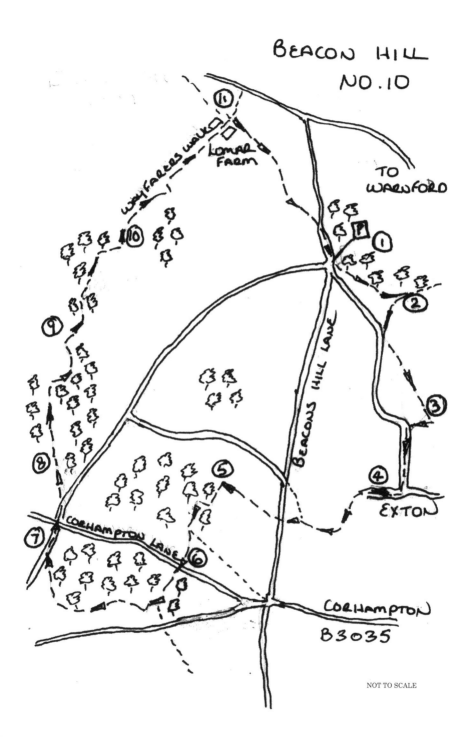

BEACON HILL
NO.10

NOT TO SCALE

53

THE WALK

1. Facing the woods, turn to your right, go through a gate and follow the track along towards the **Beacon Hill Nature Reserve**.

2. You will come across a fingerpost pointing to your right – this is the **South Downs Way**. Go through the gate and down the hill, which will lead you out onto a road. Turn left and walk down the road, and after approx 25 yards there is a fingerpost on your left, where there is also a gate. Follow the footpath along. After the footpath and down the hill you will come to a gate. Go through, and there are two more gates on your way down the hill into a field.

    Go across the field to a stile in front of you, following the **yellow markers.** Go through six stiles in total and keep following the signs. You will then come to a gate at the bottom of the field – go through and keep following the footpath.

3. When you get to the corner of the field there is a **fingerpost** saying **public footpath** and **South Downs Way.** Take the public footpath sign right, which is on the side of the fence you are standing on. There is a bungalow on your left as you walk up to the corner of the field, where you will then see a gate. Go through and out onto a road, go down the slope and bear left along the road. You will see a **vineyard** on your right. Pass the sign for **no vehicles and temp route of South Downs Way and Exton.**

4. At the bottom of the road turn right. This is **Allen Farm Lane**. This lane leads out onto a wide track with **Exton Stud** on your left. Carry along the track up a very steep hill until you meet **Beacon Hill Lane**, cross over and round a metal gate into a field, with hedges to your left.

5. Half way down the field is a large gap in the hedge. There is a sign to your left; go through the gap and turn right, and follow down into a wood.

   In the wood follow the **footpath signs**. At the sign at the bottom of the hill turn left. Once out of the woods you will come to two fields. Take the left one, following the signs, with the hedge on your right-hand side.

6. Follow the field along and you will come to **Corhampton Lane**. Cross over the lane into a small wood and follow the footpath through the woods. You will then come to a footpath going to the left and one to the right. Take the right-hand footpath. You are now walking the **Wayfarers Walk**, with a field to your left and the woods to your right. Keep on this footpath until you come to a large gate onto a road.

7. Once on the road, turn right and walk along. You will then meet the **Winchester to Droxford crossroads**. Go straight across the road heading towards **St Clair's Farm**. You will actually see a large stone with **St Clair's Farm** written on it. Turn left down this road, and follow the road around the corner, where a house called **FLINT HOUSE** will be on your left and the road turns into a track lane.

8. Follow this track all the way along. It will open out into a field with woods either side. Continue until you reach the other side and will see a sign and a gate saying **Animus Internations.** Go through the gate and follow the footpath. This wood is called **Betty Mundy's Bottom.** Keep going straight on. Keep following the hedge round, with the **yellow markers** and the large property on your left.

9. This leads you to a gate into a field. Keep to the right-hand side of the field and walk along the edge, following the signs. Following the field round to your left, after approx 50 yards you will come to a stile on your right. Go over and through the gate in front of you and follow the edge of the field, until you come to a stile on your left.

   Go through a small wood to another stile which leads into a field. Go across the field to a double set of metal gates. There is a stile, but you may be able to go through the gate.

10. Once through, bear left and follow the track. This will lead you to another track; go to your right and follow it all the way down the hill and through a gate, which then opens up into a big field. Once in the field head towards the **fingerpost** in front of you. Follow the path until you pick up a gravel track. This leads you to **Lomar Farm.**

11. On your way through the farm you will see a sign for the **South Downs Way**, follow to your right. After you

follow the track you will see another sign for the **South Downs Way** and a **drinking water tap.** Turn to your right and follow the track all the way up to the road and through the gate. You will pass **Lomer Cottage** on your right. Once on the road, turn right and walk along the road until you come to the car park, which will be on your left.

11

PEPPERBOX HILL

HISTORY:

Pepperbox Hill is a chalk ridge to the south east of Salisbury which has commanding views over the city and surrounding countryside. The Pepperbox folly was built in 1606 by Giles Eyre, supposedly for ladies to observe the hunt or for him to look down on his neighbours. It has been used by highwaymen and by the local Home Guard during World War Two.

How to get there: Pepperbox Hill is off the A36 south-east of Salisbury. From Salisbury take the A36 to Southampton. After the dual carriageway the road narrows and starts to climb. The view on your left is Pepperbox Hill. A turning left towards the car park is at the top of the incline, signposted Pepperbox Hill. From Southampton take the A36 towards Salisbury, passing through the traffic lights for Whitchurch.

Carry straight on for approx 1 mile and Pepperbox Hill is on your right on the brow of the hill.

Map Reference:	OS 131 211248
Postcode:	SP5 3QL
Where to park:	In Pepperbox hill car park
Terrain:	Fairly hilly in places
Distance:	Approx 7¾ miles
Pub:	The Red Rover. Salisbury Road, West Wellow, Romsey, Hampshire, SO51 6BW, tel: 01794 322266
Vet:	The Vets, 123 Exeter Street, Salisbury SP1 2SG, Tel: 01722 337117

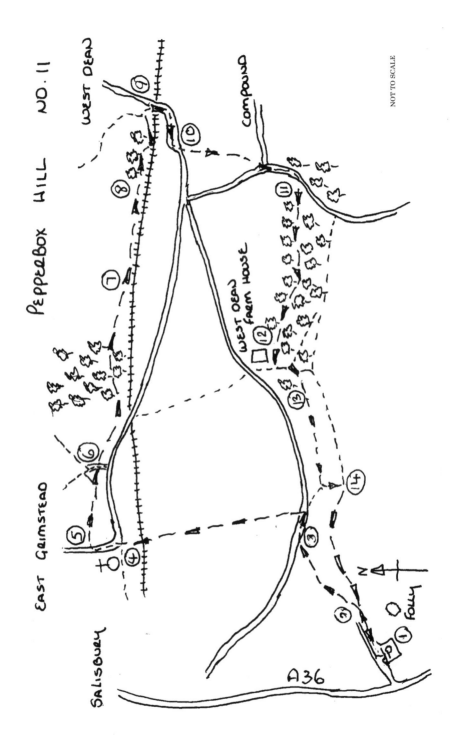

PEPPERBOX HILL NO. 11

NOT TO SCALE

THE WALK

1. Standing in the car park, with the entrance barrier to your left, in front of you is a gate and field to **Pepperbox Hill.**Follow the track with the folly on your right until you see a metal gate, and to your left is a wooden gate which goes through onto a track. Go through the wooden gate and down, turning right and follow the track.

2. At the end of the track it splits into two. Take the left track down a hill until you reach the bottom, where there is a road.

3. Turn right and walk along the road and follow for approx 175 yards to a **fingerpost** on your left, which indicates a restricted byway.

4. Follow this to the railway bridge and over until you meet a road with the **Holy Trinity Church** on the left-hand side.

5. Go straight up the road and over a bridge and after approx 100 yards on your right-hand side there is a track and **fingerpost**. Follow this up to a stile, passing **Willow Cottage**. Go over the stile and the wooden sleeper bridge. Turn to your left and go through a small opening/gate and follow the field around to your right.

   When you come to the end of the field you will see a metal gate and a small gate, where there is a **yellow marker.** Go through the small gate and follow the footpath towards a big tree in the field. Go to the left of this tree, where you will see another small metal gate. Go through into the field, keeping to the right, then go straight on until you meet a small metal gate. Go through onto a small road.

6. Go across the road to another gate. Go through and follow the right-hand side of the hedge in front of you. Follow the pylons and the footpath.

   At the end of the field you will see a big oak tree. Go to the left of the tree into the left-hand corner of the field, where you will find a gate. Go through the gate into a little wood, and take the footpath to your right, along the edge of the wood. Go through the wood and you will come to a stile. Go over and follow the footpath across the field.

7. At the end of the footpath turn left, following the edge of the field, which is parallel to the railway track. You will go straight over a track with a bridge on your right. Follow the field and it will turn to your left, due to a small stream. Follow the track until you meet a small footbridge. Go over this, turn immediately back to your right and continue following the edge of the field. Alternatively, if the stream is dry, walk straight across and follow edge of field.

8. After approx 55 yards there is a small entrance into a wood. Once in the wood, continue following the main footpath, making sure you do not go off to the right. In the middle of the wood, you will see a path leading down into a little glade and a path to your right. Follow the path to your left by the big tree, which runs parallel to the field on your left, and carry straight on.

   Go past a small lake on your left, following the main path until you get to a footbridge which goes over a stream. After crossing the footbridge, you will come to a **signpost** and a small road. Turn right and follow the road towards the railway crossing, past **St Georges Hall**, West Dean.

9. Go over the crossing and bear to your right over the bridge and go straight up the hill until you meet the national speed limit sign and the **Ordnance House** on your left.

10. Go past the sign and up a very small steep slope, which is also **signposted**. This brings you into a field with a hedge going all the way through the middle. You can go either side of the hedge, whichever you find easier. At the end of the hedgerow, follow the edge of the field, bearing right.

11. You will see a large metal gate on your left, with a track leading into a compound. Turn right and head for the road. At the road turn left and walk approx 290 yards up the road.

12. On your right will be an opening to a field with a signpost. Follow the edge of the field keeping left. At the corner of the field, bare left into woods. The path will lead you out onto a grass track by barbed wire fence and fields. (you can take the 1st footpath or follow the track to the 2nd one, but these can be overgrown).

13. Turn left and follow the track along until you reach **West Dean Farmhouse**. Follow the track past the farmhouse, which brings you through a gateway onto a little track. Turn immediately to your left and follow the track up to the footpath into woods. The footpath splits into two – follow the right-hand path. There is a sign in between the paths. Follow the **blue**

marker up the steep hill. At the top of the hill you meet another track, turn right and walk up for approx 50 yards. You will cross another track – carry on up to the top of the hill.

14. You will see a gate on your left, but follow the path to your right, which will bring you parallel to the field on your left. At the end of the footpath, the track leads up into another field. Turn directly right and follow this track. At the end, it bears to the left, up the hill, then turns right onto another path, which brings you out onto a track. Turn left and go up the hill.

15. At the top of the hill you will meet another track – turn to your right. Follow this all the way until you meet another track coming in from the right. Carry on round left and follow this track all the way back to your vehicle, which will be on your left.

12

BREAMORE ESTATE

HISTORY:

Breamore Down has many Bronze Age barrows. One is known as the Giant's Grave and is 65m long. There is a mizmaze (a maze with a distinctive pattern, only two of which remain in England) on top of the down, cut into the turf and created by either Bronze Age people or Medieval monks. Breamore Manor was once owned by Catherine Howard and also Catherine Parr, who were both queens of England. The church of St Mary dates from the Anglo-Saxon period and has been added to over the centuries. Seven double splayed Saxon windows still remain, and there is a leper window in the north wall. The four tower bells were cast in the last 16th and early 17th centuries.

Breamore House stands north-west of the church and was originally built in the 16th century. It was burnt down in 1856 and was rebuilt as a reproduction of the old building. It is privately owned but is open to visitors from April to October.

> **How to get there:** From the A338 south follow signposts to Breamore House. On your left where the road follows left, turn right and continue until you meet a crossroads. Go straight across and follow the road to St Mary's church. From the A338 north follow signposts to Breamore House on your right. Follow the road until you meet a crossroads. Turn right and follow the road to St Mary's church.

Map Reference:	OS 22 153188, OS 130
Postcode:	SP6 2DF
Where to park:	Outside St Mary's Church
Terrain:	Easy, but slight inclines
Distance:	Approx 6½ miles
Pub:	The Cartwheel Inn, Whitsbury, Fordingbridge, SP6 3PZ Tel: 01725 518362
Vet:	Forest Veterinary Clinic. 7 Park Rd, Fordingbridge SP6 1EQ Tel: 01425 652221

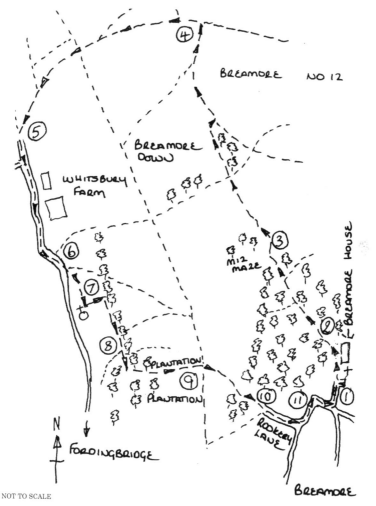

NOT TO SCALE

THE WALK

1. With your back to **St Mary's Church,** walk with the wall on your right-hand side, until you get to the automated gate. Press the button to open. Follow the road leading to a track with **Breamore House** on your right.

2. Head up the hill towards the woods. You will come to a track going left, but continue on the main track in front

of you. You will then come to another track coming in from your right and a fingerpost. Keep following the main track to your left.

3. At the end of the track it opens up into a big field. (If you go up the hill towards the trees is the ancient mizmaze). Bear to the right-hand side and there is a **waymarker** on your left. After the field carry straight on along the track. After approx 150 yards there is a **fingerpost** to Whitsbury; ignore it and carry straight on. The byway does get narrow as you continue along it.

4. You will come down to a gravel track – turn left and continue along. Keep following the track round to your left, and then you will come to a crossroads. Carry straight on up the hill, passing the gallops on your right.

5. Carry on up the hill, ignoring any fingerposts, until you meet a road. Follow the road round to the left and carry along the road/verge. Pass the cottages and **Whitsbury Farm** on your left. Once past this go up the hill, taking care on the narrow road where there is no footpath.

6. Follow the road round until you see a sign for **Whitsbury Manor & St Leonard's Church**. Turn left towards the gate, passing the sign **bridleway** on your left. Go through gate and follow the road down, following signs towards **St Leonard's Church**.

7. Before you get to the church, there is a turning to your left, going between two fields heading towards a bungalow and barns. At the bungalow, turn right and follow the track down alongside the fenced fields. Don't veer off to your left, which would lead you into the wood.

8. Keep on the main track through the woods until you

meet tracks going left, right and straight on. There are bridleway signs, but go straight on. This track leads out onto a **small plantation** on your left and right. Go straight down between the two.

9. At the bottom of this track is a gate. Go through and then right onto a large track. After approx 40 yards on your left is a sign for **footpath (please keep dogs on lead)**. Follow the footpath up the side of the field to the right-hand corner, where there is a metal gate. Go through and into a tree-lined track.

10. Follow the track down through a wooden barrier, ignoring the track to your right. Carry on straight down. The end of the track leads onto **Rookey Lane.**

11. Follow the lane till the road splits into two, and take the left-hand fork. Follow the road past **Breamore car park** on your left and to a road junction, with a sign for **Breamore & St Mary's Church**. Follow this all the way back to your vehicle.

13

UPPER CHUTE

HISTORY:

Upper Chute is a parish on the borders of Hampshire and Wiltshire. It is about six miles from Andover and is the largest village of five settlements known as "The Chutes". It did have a public house, the Cross Keys, but it is now closed. The word 'chute' is old English for forest, and Chute Forest was a royal hunting ground for William I.

How to get there: From Weyhill and the A342 head west and turn right onto Rectory Lane. After approx 3.5 miles turn left, then in approx 1.1 miles turn right into Dumner Lane. In approx 0.4 miles take a slight left onto Malthouse lane and in 0.7 miles bear left into Upper Chute and carry on to the village green on your right. Park where you can.

From Ludgershall war memorial and the A342,

head east towards Andover. After approx 0.7 miles turn left onto Biddesden Lane. In approx 1.3 miles turn left onto Newhouse lane, then in approx 1.5 miles turn left onto Forest lane. Take a slight right onto Hookwood Lane, then in approx 0.5 miles turn left onto Malthouse lane. Then bear left into Upper Chute and carry on to the village green on your right. Park where you can.

Map Reference:	OS 131 295539
Postcode:	SP11 9ER
Where to park:	Anywhere on the left, making sure all entrances are kept clear.
Terrain:	Easy, but some slight inclines and declines
Distance:	6 miles.
Pub:	The Walnut Tree, Appleshaw, nr Andover, SP11 9BN, Tel: 01264 772626
	The Hatchet Inn, Lower Chute, nr Andover, SP11 9DX, Tel: 01264 730229
Vet:	Foxcotte Vets, 15 Foxcotte Road, Chariton, Andover, SP10 4AR. Tel: 01264 358808

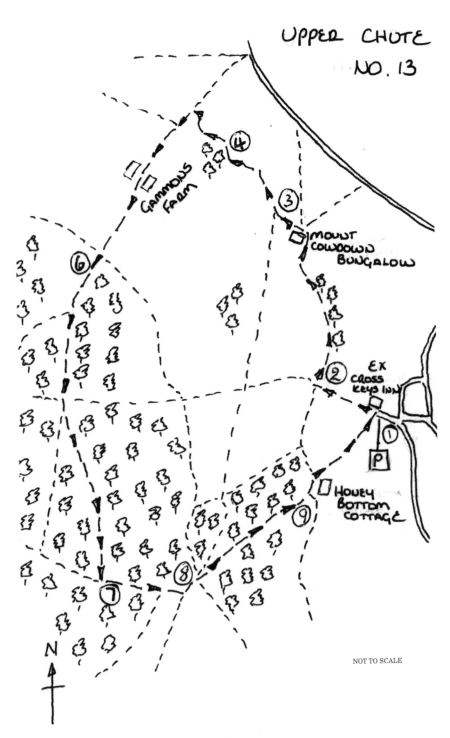

UPPER CHUTE
NO. 13

GAMMONS FARM

④

③

MOUNT
COWDOWN
BUNGALOW

⑥

②　EX
CROSS
KEYS INN

①

P

HONEY
BOTTOM
COTTAGE

⑨

⑧

⑦

N

NOT TO SCALE

72

THE WALK

1. Walk up towards the former **Cross Keys Inn** on your right-hand side. Just past the former inn, in front of you is a footpath. Follow the track down to where there is a **Restricted Byway** sign.

2. Follow the byway track to your right. Pass by a large barn and house on your left and carry on past the signs for **no motorcycles** and **no cars**. Carry on through the gates on this byway, to another track. Carry straight on up the track until you see a sign saying **Mount Cowdown Bungalow** on your left.

3. Turn left and walk past the edge of the green building/kennels on your right through to a wooded area. When you come out of the woods turn right on a track, then carry straight over another track into a small field. In the small field follow the left-hand side of the field towards a wooden gate following **Restricted Byway** sign. Once at the wooden gates, turn left and follow gravel track following the **Restricted Byway** signs. You will pass a farm building on your left and to your right is a large grassed track and a sign, follow this grassed track.

4. At the end of the grass track is a field and an opening into a wood on your left. Take that opening into the woods and follow path around. When you get to the end of the wood it brings you out to a field; t u r n right and follow the field around. Once round the field you will meet a gate on your right. Go through and turn left onto a tarmac road.

5. Follow the tarmac track down. You will go between **Gammons Farm** and farm buildings. Carry straight along the track (don't take any left-hand turns).

6. Carry straight on to **Collingbourne Wood**, ignoring tracks to the right.

7. You will come to a T-junction, turn left and follow along. After following the main track, you will come to another T-junction, turn left past the large Yew Trees.

8. After approx 75 yards you will meet another crossroads. Turn right and follow the track, going underneath pylons and all the way to the bottom.

9. At the bottom of the footpath/bridleway turn left past the house on your right, which is called **Honey Bottom Cottage**, continuing on the main gravel track up the hill. At the top of the track is a silo in front of you and sheds to your right. Turn left and carry on up the track, and it will bring you back to the former **Cross Keys.** Turn right, where you will find your parked vehicle.

14

TILSHEAD AND SALISBURY PLAIN

HISTORY:

On Salisbury Plain, the village of Tilshead lies at the head of the river Till, which is now just a small stream. It was once a Royal Borough and has two manors. Much of the land around Tilshead was bought by the War Department and is used as artillery ranges and tank training grounds. Salisbury Plain is the largest remaining area of chalk grassland in north-west Europe. It is also the largest military training area on British soil.

There is much interesting wildlife here, including many species of birds, butterflies and wild flowers. Fairy shrimps live on the plain in ruts made by the tanks which fill up with water. They are no bigger than a fingernail. They look a little bit like blades of grass in the water.

How to get there: Tilshead is situated on the A360 between Devizes and Salisbury. Opposite the Tilshead garage there is a road signposted Chitterne. Turn into that the road and in approx 30 yards is a small lay-by on your right.

Map Reference:	OS130 029479
Postcode:	SP3 4SG
Where to park:	Park in the layby on your right, which is on the road signposted **Chitterne.**
Terrain:	Easy
Distance:	Approx 5¾ miles
Pub:	The Rose & Crown. High Street, Tilshead, Salisbury SP3 4RZ Tel: 01980 621062
Vet:	Elston Veterinary Clinic, Elston Lane, Shrewton, Salisbury SP3 4HL Tel: 01980 621999

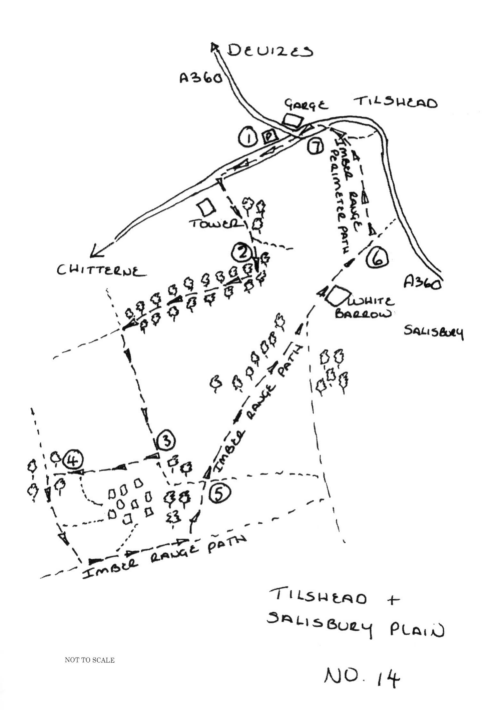

NOT TO SCALE

TILSHEAD +
SALISBURY PLAIN

NO. 14

THE WALK

1. Walk up the road toward the trees. At the top of the hill after approx 700 yards, cross the road towards a tower and go through the entrance marked **No access for civilian vehicles**. Carry straight on down the hill to your left-hand side. As the track splits into two take the right-hand one, which goes pass a water re-fuelling pipe.

2. Head up to a line of trees, and when you reach the top you will see there is an avenue of trees. Turn right and walk along the avenue. At the end of the avenue you will meet a gravel track; turn left and walk along it. Walk down the hill to the buildings in the distance.

3. When you get to the bottom of the dip you will see a **permissive byway** sign. Turn to your right and follow the track along.

4. Heading towards the trees, you will come to another track. Turn left and follow the track, which has a sign saying **permissive byway**. Keeping the village to your left, carry on past the **permissive byway** signs. Keep on the main track, which will circle the village on your left. You are now following the **Imber Range Path**. You will pass a number of **Imber Range Path** signs as you walk past the mock battle training village. Carry straight along the main track leaving the mock training village behind.

5. Continue past a small wood and down into a dip. A signpost is on your left and follow the sign for the **Imber Range**

Path. Keep following the **Imber Range Path** byway signs. Carry on down the track and in the distance, you will see **Westdown Training Camp**. This byway leads onto another byway – go to your left down the   hill   and follow this past the **Imber Range Path** signposts. As you are   going down the hill on your right-hand side is **White Barrow** (burial mound).

6. Further down there is a signpost for the **Imber Range Path**, turning to your left. This takes you across some fields. The path along the field narrows to a smaller path, with a field to your left and a shed. Carry straight along and you will come to another signpost following the **Imber Range Path**, which is also a restricted byway.

7. At the end of the path you will come to the A360. Once on the main road turn left and carry on walking. You will see **Tilshead Garage** on your right – turn left and you are back to your vehicle.

15

BISHOP'S WALTHAM

HISTORY:

Bishop's Waltham got its name through being given to The Bishop of Winchester in 904. The 'walt', meaning forest, and the 'ham', meaning settlement, were joined together to form Bishop's Waltham. It has a ruined palace built by the Bishop Henry de Blois in 1136 and destroyed by Oliver Cromwell in 1644. Much of the palace ruins were used as building materials for the town.

Bishop's Waltham was a major producer of terracotta architectural and homeware products and building brick from 1862 until 1957, when it was closed by the then owners Elliott's, but the site is now the Claylands industrial site. The town lies in the Hamble valley, which gives rise to the tributary of the River Hamble at Northbrook. Southampton, Winchester and Portsmouth are all within easy travelling distance.

How to get there: Bishop's Waltham is on the B2177 and B3035. From the west follow the B2177 Winchester road to the roundabout. Take the 1st exit signposted Corhampton on the B3035 and after approx 200 yards on the right is a lay-by which is the starting point on this walk. From the south from Waltham Chase, take the B2177 to the roundabout and take the 4th exit onto B3035. The lay-by is on your right in approx 200 yards. From Corhampton in the north east, take the B3035 to Bishop's Waltham and after Langton road on your right the layby is approx 50 yards on your left.

Map Reference:	OS 119 552177
Postcode:	SO32 1GF
Where to park:	In the layby next to the nature reserve.
Terrain:	Easy going. Can be muddy in bad weather
Distance:	Approx 6.5 miles.
Pub:	The Crown Inn, The Square, Bishop's Waltham, Southampton, SO32 1AF Tel: 01489 893350
Vet:	Animed Veterinary Hospital, Botley Road, Shedfield, Southampton SO32 2JG, Tel: 01329 833112

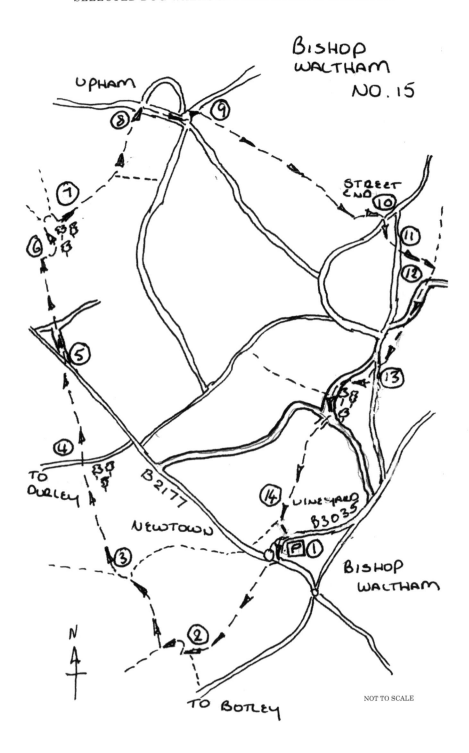

NOT TO SCALE

82

THE WALK

1. Walk towards the roundabout. Go around the roundabout until you see the **Bishop's Waltham Branch Line**, which is an old railway gate and local **Nature Reserve**. Go through and walk along.

2. At the end of the railway track it leads onto a quiet lane – turn right and follow the lane around. After approx 100 yards there is a fingerpost on your right; turn right down the track. Sign for **River View Farm**.

   Follow the track down and around, passing a pylon on your left, and through a metal gate, Following the **yellow markers**. Going on the footpath, go through the circular metal gate. Then take the left-hand path, which will lead you to another circular metal gate.

3. Once through this, turn right and follow the footpath to the right. At the end of the field you will see a wooden and a metal gate. Go through onto a track for **Tangier Farm** and turn left. After approx 20 yards there is another gate and fingerpost on your right-hand side. Go through and follow the pylons. Continue through the field until you see on your right a small bridge.

   Go across the bridge and turn immediately left, then go to the top left-hand corner of the field, where you will see two metal gates. Go through the gates keeping to the left, go straight on to another gate, and once through on your right is **Woodlea Nursery**. Follow the marker through to another gate, and then follow through the field till you get to another gate which leads onto a track for the **Woodlea Nursery**.

4. Cross the main road towards **Winters Hill Farm**. Just before the farmhouse is a **yellow sign** on your right for **public footpath**. Along the footpath you will meet a farm track. Turn immediately left, then right through a gate. This takes you onto a **Roman road** and an **information board.**

5. At the end of the **Roman Road** you will meet the **B2177**. Go across the road and turn left, then right up a small road. At the end of this road, straight in front of you is a gate. Go straight through the gate, where there is a footpath sign. Follow the footpath across the field. Bear slightly to your right at the top of the field and look to your left, and you will see a circular metal gate. Go through until you see another circular gate on your right, after a short distance of approx 100 yards. Go through and follow footpath signs across fields towards a wood.

6. When you reach the wood, turn left. After approx 100 yards there is a gap in the woods; walk through and turn left into the woods and follow the path until you get to a metal gate and a post which leads out onto a farm track.

7. Turn right down the farm track and follow all the way until you meet a metal gate. Go to the left of the metal gate, following the signs over the wooden stile. Follow the footpath and go through a circular gate.

8. Follow track past houses on your left. At the end of **Oak Close**, turn right and follow the road around into **UPHAM**. Pass the **parish church** on your left, carry on past the graveyard and down the hill, passing a duck pond on your right.

9. Following the road around to the left, after approx 60 yards from the corner on your right is a fingerpost and a metal barrier, which leads into a field. Bear to your right and go down and then up the hill until you reach a stile. Walk straight ahead till you meet a **fingerpost.** Turn left and follow that path, where you will see another **fingerpost**, which leads you past a house on your left and buildings on your right.

10. This path will lead you to a road. Cross over the road and there is a footpath sign. Go to the left of it, which takes you to a stile, then into a field. Keep to the right-hand side by the field until you meet another stile. Go over the stile and follow telegraph wires across the field to the hedge, where there is another stile, and drop down to the road.

11. Cross the road and up to another stile. Go over the stile and keep to the right-hand side of the field until you meet another stile.

12. Go over and drop down onto a track, turn right and follow it down and this leads out onto a quiet road. Carry on along the road. After going around a bend in the road, look left where there is a wooden gate and **fingerpost**, go through and follow **fingerpost**. At the end of the footpath is a gate. Go through the gate and continue on the footpath, with cottages on the left. This will bring you to a road.

13. Go across the road, and go by what looks like someone's driveway, but there is a footpath along side of the house and fingerpost. Follow the footpath, which leads between houses and a wood. At the end of the footpath is a gate, which in turns leads to a road. Turn left and follow the road down, ignoring the **restricted byway** to your right.

    Follow the lane called **Shipcote Lane** and you will meet another lane. Go straight across onto a gravel track. Carry on the track, ignoring any other signs, and go past a house called **Redhill** on your right.

14. Continue on the track, passing a vineyard on your left and a field and houses on your right. At the end of the track, which is a bridleway, you will meet a road. Turn left and down to the **B3035**. Turn right at the main road and in approx 50 yards you are back at your vehicle.

16

WHITEWOOL HANGER

HISTORY:

Whitewool Hanger is a north-east facing ridge and a favourite place for hang-gliding. Below to the west is Whitewool Pond and Meon Springs Fly Fishing. This is part of Whitewool Farm, which also has a yurt holiday village and a shepherd's hut for hire.

How to get there: Follow the A32 to Warnford and from the west turn right just after the George & Falcon onto Hayden Lane. From the east turn left, 50 yards before the George & Falcon. Continue up the hill until you meet a lane coming in from the left, Old Winchester Hill Lane. The car parking area is in front of this lane on your left.

Map Reference:	OS119 645216
Postcode:	GU32 1HW
Where to park:	Winchester Hill car park.
Terrain:	Steep decline at start and end Uneven steep incline after crossroads.
Distance:	Approx 6¾ miles
Pub:	The George & Falcon, Warnford Road, Warnford, Hampshire, SO32 3LB. Tel: 01730 829623
Vet:	St Peters Vets, 67 Portsmouth Road, Horndean, Waterlooville, PO8 9LH Tel: 02392 592526 Emergency: 01730 266431

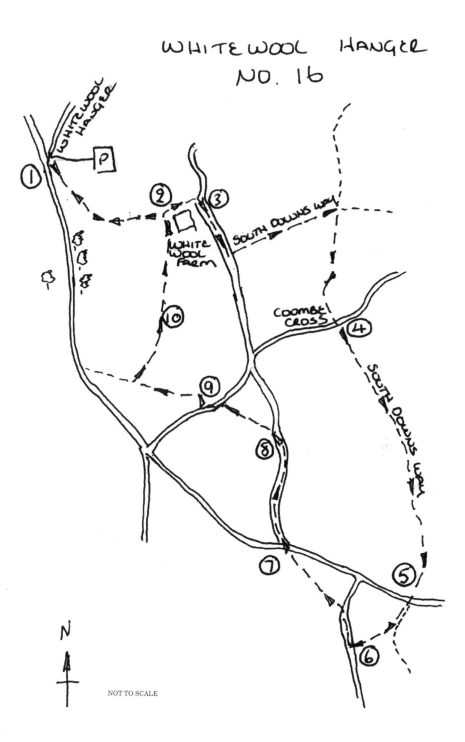

WHITEWOOL HANGER
NO. 16

NOT TO SCALE

THE WALK

1. Start at the gate and go down the hill, following the pathway. At the bottom of the hill, you will see a gate on your right-hand side. Go through this gate to another gate, approx 20 yards. Go out of the gate and follow signs for the **South Downs Way.**

2. This will lead you to **Whitewool Farm**. When you reach the farm, turn to your left and follow the road all the way to **Meon Springs Fly Fishing**. When you go over the river you will see a fingerpost on your left.

3. Turn right and follow this road for about 200-300 yards. Pass a cottage on your left, then approx 150 yards there is a fingerpost on your left for **South Downs Way**. Turn left and walk up the concrete road. At the top of the concrete road, the track merges into a grass track. Follow this and go down to the bottom, following the **South Downs Way** signs. You will come to a T junction (public byway to Butserhill). Turn right and follow all the way up the hill. This track narrows and leads to **Coombe Cross.**

4. Go straight across the road onto another track following signs for **South Downs Way**, heading towards a large communication mast. There are wonderful views at the top of the Isle of Wight.

5. At the end of the track you will meet a road. Cross the road, and on your left is **Weather Down Hostel**. You will see a fingerpost to your left – ignore that, but

JOANNE FAIREY AND MICHAEL FAIREY

slightly to your right is another fingerpost. Take the right-hand side, do not take the left side, which is a bridleway. The sign says **byway**. The footpath is to the left of a big driveway into an industrial unit.

6. At the end of the footpath, you will come out onto a small farm track. Turn right and continue. At the end of this track, follow a **restricted byway** sign leading to a footpath in front of you.

7. At the end of the footpath you will meet a road. Go across the road onto another small road, signed **Meon Springs Fly Fishing**.

8. After approx 800 yards down this road is a signpost to your left saying **footpath**. Go through the gate and follow edge of field. Once through the fields you will meet a double metal gate leading onto a small road. Go through gate and turn left, and after approx 70 yards there is a **fingerpost** on your right.

9. Go through the gate, following the edge of the field. On your right you will come to another gate. Once through the gate/stile follow signs to **Monarch Way**. Cross the field until you reach a stile/fence, turn right and head towards **Castle Cottages**, which lead onto a farm track. Just before you get to the cottages, go through a metal gate with a **yellow marker sign**.

10. Go straight onto the farm track leading back to **Whitewool Farm**. Follow the track until you reach the farm and follow **yellow markers** through the farm yards. At the end of farm buildings there is a **yellow**

marker on your right-hand side, pointing left. This will take you to the track from which you originally started. Go through the gates up the hill back to your car park.

17

WESTWOOD

HISTORY:

The Farley Mount short walk takes you around the perimeter of part of the Westwood, which is a forest and nature reserve near the village of Sparsholt. It is an ancient woodland and is owned and managed by the Forest Commission. It covers approx 25 hectares of woodland and starts just 2.5 miles west of Winchester.

How to get there: Farley Mount is to the west of Winchester. From the M3 exit at junction 11 onto A3090 towards Winchester/St Cross. At the roundabout take 2nd exit onto Badger Farm Road A3090 signposted Romsey. At the next roundabout stay on the A3090. At roundabout take 1st exit onto A3090. Down the hill and turn right onto Enmill Lane. In approx 1.2 miles at the T junction, turn right onto

Sparsholt Road. At the crossroads turn left, signposted Kings Sombourne. Follow this road to a T-junction and then turn right. Take the 2nd car park on your right, called 'Hawthorn'.

Map Reference:	OS132 413293
Postcode:	SO21 2JG
Where to park:	Hawthorn Car park
Terrain:	Easy
Distance:	Approx: 2.5 miles
Pub:	The Dolphin Inn, Main Road, Hursley, SO21 2JY, Tel: 01962 775209
Vet:	Mildways Veterinary Centre, Easton Lane, Winchester, SO23 7RU Tel: 01962 854088

WEST WOOD
NO. 17

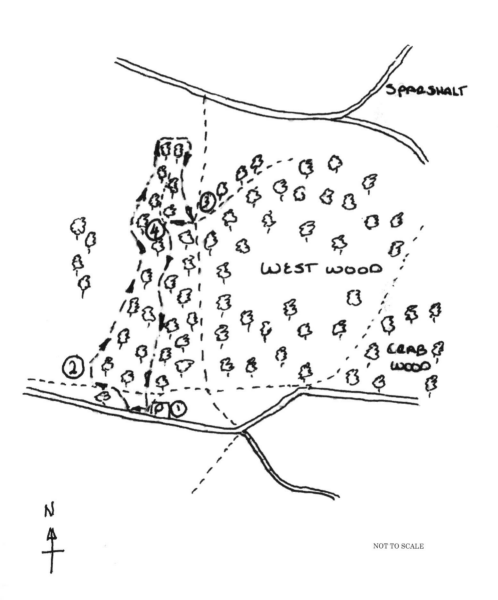

N

NOT TO SCALE

THE WALK

1. Facing the road, turn to your right and follow the **Clarendon Way** sign. When you reach a gate and a field beyond, turn to your right and follow the fence all the way along until you meet a gate in front of you, ignoring any gates to the left. Go through this gate.

2. After approx 150 yards there is another gate on your right, leading into the woods. Follow this path through the woods, keeping the fields to your left. Ignore any paths coming in from your right.

3. Continue keeping the fields to your left until you come out onto a main track, then follow the main track to your right. Follow this track until you meet another track coming down from the right-hand side.

4. Go up this track, which is on a slight incline, and walk through the woods until this track meets another track. Turn left and continue all the way up, ignoring any paths coming from your left and right. Continue up past the barriers, which in turn bring you back to your vehicle.

18

MANOR FARM

HISTORY:

Manor Farm Country Park is owned by Hampshire County Council and is a site of historic interest throughout. The *Grace Dieu,* which was the flagship of Henry V of England, was moored up at anchor when she was hit by lightning and burned. The remains are still in the River Hamble opposite the parks pontoon; a yellow marker buoy marks their position in the river. During the Second World War the area of the country park was designated as a naval base called HMS *Cricket.* From 1943 until 1946 it was used as a Royal Marine landing craft training base. The base was later used to assemble troops and landing craft for the D-Day landings. The docking jetties and many of the bases of the buildings can be seen at various places and along the river throughout the park. After the war the base was used to accommodate homeless people from Southampton.

How to get there: From junction 7 of the M27, take the signpost to Manor Farm and Hamble River Country Park. At the roundabout take the first exit up and over the hill sign posted Hedge End & Botley. At the bottom of the hill take the first turning on your right, which is Heath House Lane, and continue on the road until you meet a T junction. Turn left, and after a gradual left-hand bend you will see yellow marker posts on your left. Turn right into a car park marked 'Norman Rodaway Pavilion' and a children's park and stride sign.

Alternatively, at the roundabout for Manor Farm & Hamble River Country park, take the second exit through the new housing estate, which will take you over a bridge. Continue along the road until you see the yellow marker post on your left, where you will turn right.

If you're travelling in from Botley, at the roundabout take the first exit and go straight on through two roundabouts. At the third take the first exit and on your left is Norman Rodaway Pavilion.

Map Reference:	OS119 495119
Postcode:	SO30 0LE
Where to park:	Rodaway Pavilion
Terrain:	Easy, with slight inclines
Distance:	Approx 3.3 miles
Pub:	The Railway Inn, Station Hill, Curdridge, Southampton, SO30 2DN Tel: 01489 874226

Vet: Hedge End Veterinary Centre,
38 Wildern Lane, Hedge
End, Southampton, SO30 4EH
Tel: 01489 782317

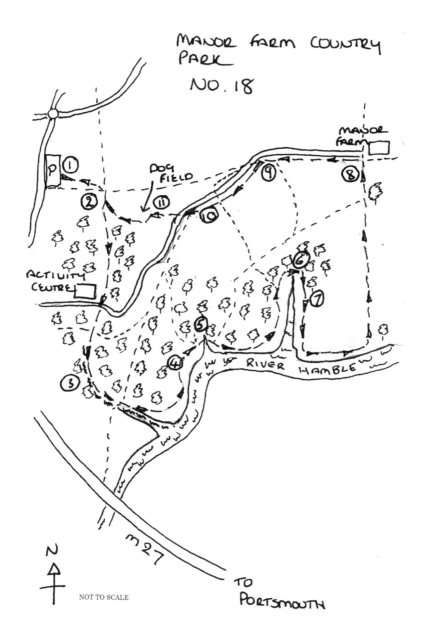

99

THE WALK

1. Starting at Norman Rodaway Pavilion car park, walk across the recreation ground to the right-hand corner. There is an entrance between the hedges. Go through the barriers on to a lane, turn left, and just past **Tansfield Stud** on your right, there is a metal gate with a yellow marker sign.

2. Once through the gate you are in Manor Farm Country Park. Carry on this track until you meet a road, ignoring any tracks to your left and right. This little road leads onto the **Queen Elizabeth Activity Centre** on your right. Carry straight on and in approx 50 yards is a track on your left. Follow this till you meet main Manor Farm Road. Go straight across, through the gap and then bear to your left. Follow the track down. Wen you meet another track you will see a poo bin – turn to your right. Carry on down the track with a signposted toilets/picnic area to your left, but carry straight on.

3. You are now following a stream on your right-hand side. Continue along the main track, ignoring any other track to your right or left. You are now following the River Hamble upstream. To your right you will see a pontoon and **information boards**, also a **yellow buoy** indicating the wreck of the *Grace Dieu*. Carry along the track, following various marker signs, past another   information board and a seat.

4. Approx 50 yards on, there is a set of steps going down to the beach on your right. If the tide is too high, follow

the hide tide path adjacent to the beach, otherwise, go down to the beach and turn left. The beach gives you wonderful views of the River Hamble.

After you have walked along the beach you will see another set of steps and a seat. Go up the steps, and half way up, you will meet the hide tide path coming in from your left. Turn to your right and there you will see the sign of a strawberry. At the end of the track you will meet one of the main tracks coming in. Turn to your right and walk up the small hill.

Follow the river to your right. You will come to a crossroads where there is a tree which has been cut down and made into a seat.

5. Turn to your right, go down the steps, over the bridge and up the other side. At the top the paths divide left and right – take the right path, following the river. Looking to your right all the way along the river bank, there are cut-outs that were used to house the landing craft for the D-Day invasion in 1944.

6. Carry on along the main path over another small bridge and continue along the main track, ignoring any track to your right or left.

7. At the end of the track it branches left and right. Take the right-hand track down some steps and over another bridge. Walk up the hill to your right through the woods, now following the stream to the river.

8. At the end of the wood are a couple of openings that leads into a field. Follow the footpath down towards the pine trees and the river Hamble. Follow the edge of the field all the way round till you pass a large oak tree and a gateway. Carry straight on a wide track with fields to your left and right, belonging to Manor Farm.

9. You will come to a set of gates and a single gate. Go through the single gate (Manor Farm is to your right – they serve refreshments there. Dogs are not allowed in the farm itself or the café, but welcome in the refreshment area). Then turn left and walk down the track.

10. The road is on your right-hand side. Continue walking parallel to the road, and go through a double gate. 20 yards after the gate is a sign on your left saying **Manor Farm, tea rooms and toilets. Barnfield, toilets.**

11. When you meet a junction with the road to the right, and a track coming in from the left, carry straight on until you come to another fingerpost, saying **Manor Farm &, tea rooms ½ mile Barnfield, toilets** and a gap in the hedge, turn to your right and go straight across the road and through a gate into the BBQ field.

12. Carry straight on to the top of the field, turn to your left and walk through a gate into a car park. Carry on walking through the car park and on your right is an enclosed dog field, then a car park ticket machine. Just after the machine is a path into the woods on your

right. Go over a small bridge and one step, turn to your right and follow the track until it meets another track. Turn to your right and walk up to the metal circular gate, then back into Rodaways recreation ground and back to your vehicle.

19

CHERITON WALK

HISTORY:

Cheriton is a small village and parish near Alresford in Hampshire. It is famous for being the source of the River Itchen and the battle of Cheriton in 1644 during the English Civil War. Cheriton has two pubs, one being the Flower Pots Inn, which brews its own beer and has won numerous awards over the years. The church dates from the 12th century and is called St Michael and All Angels.

How to get there: Cheriton is off the A272 north west of Hinton Ampner. Turn onto the B3046 and follow road through village until you see a village green with a memorial. Turn right and follow this road for approx 200 yards, when you will see a small bridge on your right. Turn right over the bridge and right again into a cul de sac with a stream running beside the road.

Map Reference:	OS132 583285
Postcode:	SO24 0QA
Where to park:	In the cul de sac by Cheriton Primary School.
Terrain:	Moderate hills at Hinton Ampner, but easy going after. Can be muddy in bad weather.
Distance:	Approx 7.5 miles
Pub:	The Hinton Arms. Petersfield Road, Cheriton, Alresford, Hampshire, SO24 0NH, Tel: 01962 771252
Vet:	Cedar Veterinary Group, The Veterinary Surgery, New Farm Rd, Alresford SO24 9QW, Tel: 01962 732535

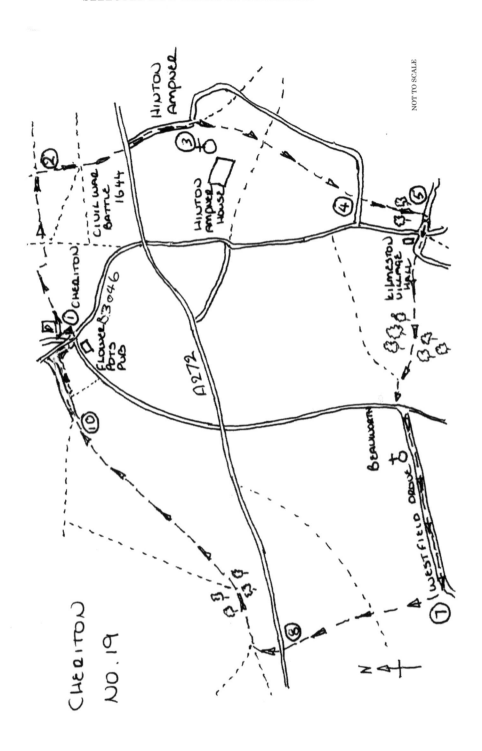

THE WALK

1. Walk towards the end of the cul de sac, where on the left is a signpost saying **Wayfarers Walk**, on a wooden fence. Walk up the footpath, and it will narrow out onto a field. Follow the signs. At the end of the field you will go through a gap where there is a stile; you will meet a crossroads. Carry straight on where a sign says **restricted byway**.

2. You will meet a lane called the **Wayfarers Walk.** Turn to your right and over the hill and follow the lane down, going underneath a metal barrier. Before you get to the **A272**, on your left is Primrose Cottage and on your right is an information board about **The English Civil War, battle of Cheriton 1644.**

   When you get to the main road, go across and up the hill. Head up towards **Hinton Ampner.**

3. At the top of the road, bear to your right for **Wayfarers Walk.** Go through a set of large metal gates. On your right is **All Saints parish church**. After approx 50 yards on your left-hand side is a fingerpost and a set of gates. Once through the gates, follow the path to your right and go down the hill. **Hinton Ampner House** is now on your right-hand side.

   At the end of the track go through two gates, following the **Wayfarers Walk** and **National Trust** signs across the fields. You will come to a gate with more **National Trust** signs. Go through the gate and across a field until you come to a stile. Go over the stile and follow the footpath to the right-hand side of the field.

4. Once across the field you will reach another stile which leads onto a small road. Cross the road and turn to your right. After approx 20 yards on your left-hand side is a **Wayfarers** marker. The signpost is opposite **Kilmeston Manor** entrance. Go over a stile and follow the footpath to the right of the field.

   Following the **Wayfarers** marker, go over another stile and follow the footpath into a small patch of woodland, which will then lead to another stile and a track. Go over this and into a small wood. Once through the wood you will come to a gate with the **Wayfarer** markers on it. Go through and across a track to another gate.

5. After about 20/30 yards you will meet a road. Turn right and carry on up the road, past two sets of cottages and you will come to another road. In front of you is a **Wayfarer** marker. **Do not follow it**, but bear to your right towards the thatched cottage and past **Kilmeston Village Hall**.

   Turn left across the green to another road, signed posted **Bishop's Waltham** and **Winchester**. After a short walk along the road you will see a speed limit sign, and on your right-hand side is a track, turn right down the track going between two fields. This track leads into a wood. Keep following the footpath signs.

   Carry on this track up the hill until you meet a stile, then go over the stile into a field. Follow the signs across two small fields and three stiles. After the last stile turn to your left, follow the edge of the field down to the road, and with the church in front of you, you will come to a metal gate.

6. Once through onto the road, turn left. You will then come to **BEAUWORTH**, a small village green – turn to your right. Go up past some thatched cottages and **St James' Church** on your right. Walk along **West Field Drove** past **Hamilton Farm**, and carry on straight up the road.

7. When you come to a left-hand bend in the road, there is a marker post on your left. Turn to your right in front of the barn and follow **Holden Lane** (track) all the way along.

8. Along this track you will meet another track, which is the South Downs Way. Carry straight across this and carry on walking, going through **Holden Farm,** which brings you up to the **A272**.

9. Cross the road and go up the hill until you meet a gate, following all the signs to the **South Downs Way**. When you reach the gate go through and turn right through the field, continuing along the **South Downs Way**. You will get to another metal gate and into a little wood and a sign saying **bridleway.** Through the wood you will come to a sign saying **restricted byway** – turn to your left.

After approx 30 yards, you will see more signs and a stile on your right. Go over the stile into the field. Head towards the right-hand corner of the field, which brings you to a V-shaped barrier. Go through it and follow the footpath sign.

10. This footpath leads you onto a concrete track. Continue on this track, past houses to your left, until you reach a footpath sign to your right. Turn right into the field and then turn immediately left and follow the left-hand edge of the field. Follow the outside of the field all the way down and past a children's play area on your right. Follow the narrow footpath and walk alongside the recreation field. Carry on walking on the left until you reach a small footpath on your left.

11. Follow this onto the road towards the village with the **Flower Pots** pub in front to you. Turn left down the road till you get to the bottom. At the bottom turn to your right and approx 50 yards, just before **Cheriton House** on your left, is a footpath sign. Turn left and follow the stream all the way back to your vehicle.

20

SHAWFORD & COMPTON

HISTORY:

Shawford is part of the Parish of Compton and Shawford in the city of Winchester. It is most notable for its station and film set. Victor Meldrew's death in 'One foot in the Grave' was filmed under the railway bridge and the 1974 remake of 'Brief Encounters' starring Sophia Loren was partly filmed in the station. The river Itchen runs through the village, which has the longest railway viaduct in Hampshire. There is one pub in Shawford, the Bridge Inn, which sits beside the River Itchen. The villages of Compton and Shawford are separated by the Shawford Downs and also the M3 motorway.

How to get there: Shawford lies between Winchester in the north, Twyford in the east, Otterbourne in the south and Compton in the west. From the south leave the M3 at junction 11, taking the A3090 exit to

Winchester. At the roundabout take the second exit onto the Hockley Link A3090. At the next roundabout take the first exit onto Otterbourne Road. Over the motorway bridge and turn left into Shawford Road. Go down the hill, and before the station on your right is a nature reserve car park.

From Twyford in the east take the Shawford Road and go under the railway bridge and slightly up the hill with the nature reserve car park on your left

Map Reference:	OS 132 471249
Postcode:	SO21 2AA
Where to park:	In the nature reserve car park.
Terrain:	Easy going, but slightly hilly towards the end.
Distance:	Approx 5 miles.
Pub:	The Bridge Inn, Shawford Road, Shawford, Hampshire, SO21 2BP. Tel: 01962 713171
Vet:	Stable Cross Veterinary Centre, St Cross Road, Winchester, SO23 9PR Tel: 01962 841001/840505

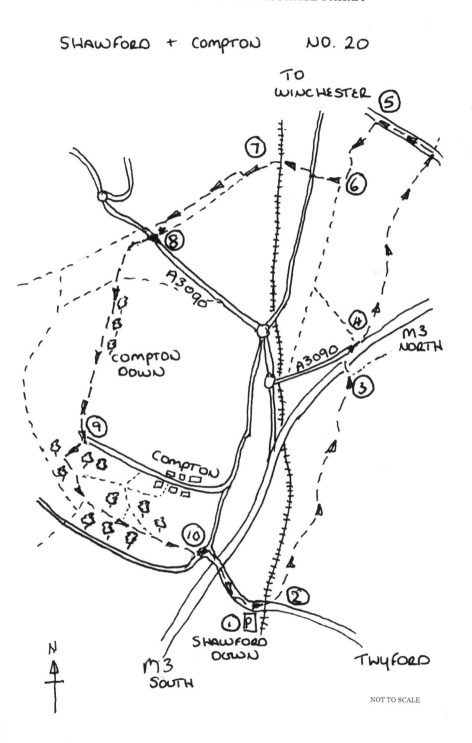

SHAWFORD + COMPTON   NO. 20

TO WINCHESTER ⑤

⑦

⑥

⑧

A3090

⑭

M3 NORTH

COMPTON DOWN

A3090

③

⑨

COMPTON

⑩

②

① P

SHAWFORD DOWN

M3 SOUTH

TWYFORD

N

NOT TO SCALE

THE WALK

1. Head out towards the road, and there is a path leading down towards the station. Go under the railway bridge and pass the **Bridge Inn** pub on your left.

2. Go over the river bridge and cross the road to your left, following the **Itchen Navigation** footpath beside the river. You will come to a gate. Go through and continue following the river along the **Itchen Way**. Go through another gate, which takes you through **Hockley Meadows Nature Reserve**. Continue following the path through to another gate, following the **Itchen Way**. Go through another gate and over a little bridge and continue following the river.

3. The path then splits into two – take the left-hand path over the   bridge. Go underneath the motorway bridge and follow the path up to the main **A3090** road.

4. Cross the road and turn right, then left onto a path. Follow the path signposted for the **Itchen Navigation**. Go underneath a disused railway bridge, follow the path, and looking to your right you will see **St Catherine's Hill**. Just after the entrance to **St Catherine's Hill** on your right is a signpost for you to turn left down to a path alongside the river.

    At the end of the footpath is a car park on your right and a bridge in front of you, go up onto the road a turn left. Walk along the footpath by the road, and at a point along the road, cross over and follow the path.

5. After approx 550 yards you will see a sign on your right for **St Cross Hospital**. Cross over the road and follow the path, signposted **Clarendon Way** and **Pilgrims Trail**. Following this track, **St Catherine's Hill** is now on your left in the distance. Continue along this path until you meet a gate.

6. Go through the gate and in front of you is the hospital of **St Cross,** founded in 1132. Go over the wooded bridge and head towards the right-hand corner of the wall. Go through the wooden gate, walking alongside the hospital.

    Walk up to the road, with the **Bell Inn** on your left-hand side, cross the road, turn to your right, and take the first turning on your left, which is **Mead Road.** Walk up the road to the bridge over the railway.

7. Go over the railway bridge and at the bottom is a sign **Valley of Fields**. Follow the signs straight up the track. As you go up through the track on your right-hand side are numerous gates to go into a meadow. Once into the meadow, turn left and keep going through gates until you reach the very end, where you will meet another wooden gate. Go through and turn to your left. There is an information slab showing you where various points are in Winchester. Then walk up till you meet a metal barrier and turn to your right and down to the **A3090**.

8. Cross over the road and go up the track in front of you, which is a restricted byway.Carry straight on past

any signs. After approx 200 yards, you will come to a crossroads in the path. Carry straight on, with a field to your right and an avenue of trees to your left.

9. Along the track you will see on your right a signpost saying **Restricted Byway.** Follow the footpath to your right into the woods. Continue until you come to signs pointing to your left and straight on. Follow the track straight on and the path leads up to your right, where there is a gate. Go through the gate into a field and bear to your left, following the footpath.

   At the bottom left hand side of the field is another gate. Go through the gate and turn right back through the woods. You will be following the footpath parallel to the road on your right. This brings you down onto a wider footpath. Go down the slope and turn right, then immediately left on another track, signposted **Valley of Fields**.

   Keep following the **yellow marker**, which leads to a metal barrier. You will then meet another track. Go to your right, past the steps up the hill.

10. The track will bring you down to a double set of metal gates. Go through the gates and over the road onto a footpath, then turn to your left and follow this path to a road over the motorway bridge.

    Walk over the motorway bridge and turn left over the road towards **Shawford** and **Shawford Station**. Walk down the road and back to your vehicle.

Printed in Great Britain
by Amazon